ROBERT
VAN GULIK
HIS LIFE HIS WORK

Robert Hans van Gulik, Ambassador of the Netherlands

ROBERT VAN GULIK
HIS LIFE HIS WORK

Janwillem van de Wetering

Introduction by Arthur P. Yin

Published by Soho Press, Inc.
853 Broadway
New York, NY 10003

Cover illustration and illustration on page 52
by Joe Servello.

Library of Congress Cataloging-in-Publication Data
Van de Wetering, Janwillem, 1931–
Robert van Gulik : his life, his work /
Janwillem Van de Wetering.
    p.   cm.
Originally published: Miami Beach :
D. McMillan Publications, 1987
Includes bibliographical references.
ISBN 1-56947-124-X (alk. paper)
1. Gulik, Robert Hans van, 1910–1967.
2. Authors, Dutch—20th century—Biography.
3. Ambassadors—Netherlands—Biography.
I. Title.
PT5838.G9Z94   1998
823′.914—dc21
[B]   98-15703
CIP

ROBERT
VAN GULIK
HIS LIFE HIS WORK

Also by the author

For Joe Brumit

Introduction

Robert van Gulik loved the traditional Chinese novels that I read when I was growing up in rural Hong Kong in the early 1950s. *The Romance of the Three Kingdoms, The Water Margin*, and *Ch'I Hsia Wu I (The Seven Heroes and the Five Righteous)* were read by every Chinese boy of my generation. These stories were also the basis for local theatrical performances and comic strip serials; their heroes were pictured in cheap prints that we avidly collected. It was through reading these works that we became acquainted with the traditional Chinese tribunal ruled by a magistrate, in his winged cap, surrounded by his retinue of court personnel. They were the inspiration for our games in which we were brave "Brothers of the Green Woods" or members of the Beggars Guild who hated "dog" officials.

The China that van Gulik had lived in, in which I spent my childhood, was a country in transition. The New Territories of Hong Kong still had verdant vegetable fields tended by hand. We swam in natural watering holes and caught shrimp with our bare hands. Water buffalo, peasants, temples, Buddhist monks, bamboo groves: these were everyday sights. This was the age-old Chinese landscape that resonates in Chinese poetry and ci (tze) which were then still being taught to schoolchildren. There were feudal remnants in society as well. Occasionally, old ladies

hobbled along on bound feet; some of the mothers of my
classmates were concubines. Storytellers riveted our attention with tales of ghosts from *Liao Chai Chih I (Strange
Stories from a Chinese Studio)*. Walking home from the
city on festival days we would try to blow out the flames of
one another's lanterns with which we were lighting our
way and frighten each other by reenacting these ghost stories. Our schooltexts emphasized patriotism and we were
inculcated with a keen sense of morality, of righteousness.
And I had personal experiences evoking the traditional
Chinese sensibility such as being awakened amidst much
excitement in the middle of one night by our Buddhist nun
neighbors and following them groggily to bear witness to
the blooming of flowers that occurred only once a decade. I
still remember the fragrance.

It was also a period of transiency. People who succeeded in reaching Hong Kong after the wars were unde-
cided about their next step. Some left for Taiwan, some
returned to the Mainland. Those who stayed made nu-
merous moves before settling down. Some of my teachers
had been scarred by their wartime experiences. Occasionally we witnessed people going mad, screaming, with
untied hair, wielding a cleaver (a traditional Chinese display of madness).

But when my family emigrated to the United States
when I was eleven the cultural influences that had formed
me receded from my life.

Some twenty-five years later I discovered the Judge
Dee mysteries. And here, in plain English, was all my
Chinese past, personal and literary, once more evoked.
The old Chinese locutions: "this insignificant person"; the
food: the oily onion cake and jugs of wine that Ma Joong
and Chiao Tai enjoy; the traditional Confucian enemies

of literature: the nefarious meat-eating Buddhist monks. And these mysteries, particularly the earlier ones, not only followed the traditional forms but displayed the social sensibilities peculiar to the China of feudal times as seen, for example, in the intricate play of feelings between Judge Dee and Mrs. Kuo of *The Chinese Nail Murders*; the terrible, utterly ruthless vendetta extending for nearly thirty years of *The Chinese Bell Murders*; the tea ceremony described by Master Crane Robe in *The Chinese Maze Murders*. These mysteries transport us back in time and place; and the solutions to the crimes in the cases brought before Judge Dee are integral to the society over which he presides.

I was immediately hooked by the Judge Dee mysteries which had brought back to me so much that I had nearly forgotten. I can only assume that their appeal for those who have no Chinese cultural roots is similarly based; they convincingly set before the reader a world that has now vanished, or at the least been overlain. And they do so in a form which is popular and accessible.

Once hooked, I became curious about the creator of these mysteries. From the postscripts, and from Donald Lach's introduction to some of the earlier reprints, I learned that van Gulik had been a dedicated Sinologist. About ten years ago I acquired a copy of the earlier edition of Janwillem van de Wetering's biography of Robert van Gulik which informed me about van Gulik's Japanese background and his knowledge of Zen Buddhism as well as of Taoism. This scholarly man, born in The Netherlands, has been fortunate in his biographer. For van de Wetering, too, is Dutch by birth and by inclination a student of Eastern culture and religion. And he, too, has earned international renown for a series of mysteries which reveals to the astute reader a philosophy that informs its principal characters' lives and provides them with the means of solving the mysteries they confront.

I am honored to have been asked to introduce to new readers this biography of Robert van Gulik, a man who has given so much information and pleasure to so many readers of the Judge Dee mysteries, by Janwillem van de Wetering, his worthy follower.

Arthur P. Yin,
Glendale, California

1

Omaidasu to wa (Remembering)

To remember
Is to forget again
Don't remember
So you won't have to forget

A Japanese poem, translated by Dr. R. H. van Gulik
(1910–1967), mainly known as the author of sixteen detective novels featuring the legendary Chinese magistrate, Judge Dee.

A most extraordinary man, this Robert van Gulik, and
I don't remember him for we never met. Even so, I know
him well.

It's my own fault I never met him for we were in some
of the same countries at some of the same times, but I
avoided a personal confrontation with a cherished author. A reader easily creates a writing god, and elevates

another mortal man onto a high pedestal. A meeting in
the flesh may cause a fall and the pain of disappoint-
ment. The veils of fantasy rip and there is the harsh
glare of reality again. But then, who is to say that there
is no reality in fantasy? Here the good doctor is, looking
at me from his framed portrait on my altar, through little
round glasses. The expression he assumes for the moment is fairly severe. His tie and shirt balloon uncom-
fortably—the lines connecting chin and mouth are tightly
drawn. He wasn't happy and people who knew him during that period knew why. Too many official duties, red
tape to be ceremoniously cut, too much theft of his private time. He was Dutch Ambassador to Japan and, although the appointment crowned his career, it was hard
for him to retain equanimity when each day would bring
his secretary and the secretary would bring a list.

"Sir."
"Yes."
"Your Excellency."
"Yes, yes."
"There will be a reception, Your Excellency, this afternoon."
"Ah."
"And before that an official lunch."
"Ah, yes."
"And tonight there will be an official dinner."
"Yes."
"And in about an hour there will be a preview of Dutch
export cheese in a ship, your limo is waiting."
"Yesyes*YES*."

Here again, reality versus cherished fantasy.
Van Gulik had other plans for the day. He would wan-

der off into Tokyo's back alleys, peruse reasonably priced antiques, observe the *couleur locale* of one of this planet's most exotic and overcrowded capitals. Had he studied the Horse Cult of Tibet to look at *cheese*?

He wanted to look at the delicate geishas tripping along on high wooden sandals.

The secretary knew how van Gulik hated the daily destruction of his dream, but he had to go into the study and remind his employer of his duties.

At that time the Judge Dee mysteries became world famous and fans tried to seek van Gulik out, to express admiration and to ask a hundred questions. A friend of mine managed to penetrate the embassy's defenses, and van Gulik walked him up and down courtyards and gardens, attached to the luxurious mansion housing top Dutch diplomats assigned to Japan. Together they enjoyed the evening song of the gibbons van Gulik liked to keep; agile and polite primates, originating in China. Van Gulik sang with the monkeys, in a strong baritone. He also played the seven stringed Chinese lute and showed my friend his art collection. He didn't answer his hundred questions.

I met a man who worked under van Gulik during less busy times, where van Gulik was temporarily stationed back home in The Hague. He was in charge of Dutch affairs in the Middle East and sundry African nations, and maybe not too much was going on. This was his routine. He showed up at 9 a.m. sharp every day and 'perused' his mail (picking it up? putting it down?). Then he dictated some answers. Then, refusing coffee, he strolled off to the station, caught a train, sat in the train for twenty minutes while reading a Chinese treatise on a 'lesser subject.' (He specialized in trivia, keeping away from 'the central tradition,' from the great problems of Chinese history and society; he avoided philosophy). He left the train at Leyden and walked over to the university. There he finally had his morning coffee, and, with fresh energy, pored over tomes, searched libraries, checked art collections. The calligraphy of his notes could not be faulted. Four p.m. sharp found him back at his governmental desk again, to sign the letters he had dictated earlier on. He would listen to *brief* (the briefer the better; he kept telling his co-workers that no words are wasted in a Chinese poem) reports on the international situation, that as Tom Robbins points out these days, is always as desperate as ever, then walked home. At home waited more study, at his desk, in his library, between his art treasures. He wrote, and also illustrated both his scholarly dissertations and his (only partly) fictitious novels. He did different work during his breaks.

The official residence the Dutch government let him live in had a heating problem. Several old-fashioned stoves were being temperamental in the basement. Van Gulik analysed their emotions and tended them lovingly, feeding each stove its favorite mix of coal that he shoveled himself. Doing hard labor, he told his family, relaxed his mind. Not having much need of sleep, he would spend most of the night in his study, writing a Chinese treatise in Chinese, practising Arab and Sanskrit scripts, sketching a plot for yet another Judge Dee novel, drawing a naked lady in the style popular during the Ming dynasty. He did die down for a few hours, enjoyed his morning shower and shave, fixed his own breakfast and strolled back to work.

He was not a full-time hermit. A wife, three sons and a daughter required some time. He also conversed with his

monkeys, that would startle visitors by their sudden appearance. He even socialized. There were elegant dinner
parties, specializing in Chinese delicatessen. Mrs. van
Gulik is Chinese, the daughter of a Chinese diplomat,
later mayor of Tsientsin. They met during WW II in
Chunking, where his future wife was working at the
Dutch embassy.

After dinner Dr. van Gulik escorted his male guests to
his study, where he poured cognac in crystal tumblers,
handed out prize cigars, worked up a few jokes, then introduced the *pièce de résistance* of that evening's entertain-
ment: an elaborate display of his erotic art collection. There
were prints and paintings, risqué poetry to be recited, and
there were ivory eggs, that unscrewed, and contained
screwing miniatures, most delicately sculpted. Van Gulik
also liked to go to the movies. Kids like to go to movies and
the van Gulik kids had, in this respect, an ideal father. He
would go anywhere to see a good picture, or even a bad picture, for 'badness is merely reversed good.' How not to show
things, he sometimes liked to be shown.

And he liked to travel—not just big travel, part of being sent to one country after another, but little trips, the
small movements within an overall known space. A con-
sular clerk who once served under van Gulik told me
about his chief's reputation in Malaysia. He simply
wouldn't be at his desk, which angered the big boss.
"Where?" the ambassador would thunder, but nobody
ever knew. "Increasing my knowledge, sir," van Gulik
would mumble, being questioned as to his whereabouts
upon his return. Then he would hold forth on the useless-
ness of foreign officials who have no idea of what the
country they are posted to is like. Who couldn't even
speak the language. Who knew nothing of the culture.

"How," van Gulik would emphasize, pounding his superior's desk, "can men like you and me be expected to serve our country's interests if we merely sit here and answer the phone?"

"But what did he do?" I asked my informant.

He didn't know. "Maybe sex," he thought. "Van Gulik *was* interested in sex, you know. He wrote dissertations on the subject."

I insisted on details. There weren't any. The doctor was reputed to travel alone, staying in native inns, eating local foods, listening to story tellers, checking what was on sale in small stores and market stalls.

"The colleagues frowned on such pursuits, but they couldn't stop him. He was important long before he got to the top. Nobody messed with our scholar."

But then, of course, the doctor *was* a scholar, who truly penetrated every country he happened to be in. With his phenomenal talent for language analysis and pronunciation (although he always inserted his own Dutch accent) he could crack the new code, and gain entry into both past and present culture. Equipped with a curiosity that went into many directions at once he would study local law (colonial law had been a part of his studies in Leyden). He also sampled local musical instruments, and in China began to play the seven stringed lute. He paid attention to all types of wildlife, and if there were any monkeys around he'd be sure to look them up. His last treatise, *The Gibbon In China,* is a fascinating study for at least several reasons and will be referred to more fully later on.

Van Gulik's charismatic personality and imposing stature plus his amazing gifts for picking up language and lore made him famous wherever he went, but true worldwide fame accrued from his Judge Dee saga. As the author of this most popular series of classic Chinese thrillers he literally reached millions, in over ten countries, including myself, despairing at that time* in a Japanese Zen monastery's dusty backroom. It seems to be a part of Zen training that the students are discouraged to read, and even simple everyday questions will not be answered by their tutors. Sitting still for many hours each day was beginning to bore me and I disliked the beatings that were supposed to cheer up my sluggish mind. The food wasn't anything to write home about either. I had escaped into a library (for advanced students, as I found out later) and came across van Gulik's translation of an authentic Chinese thriller, *Dee Goong An,* featuring several cases solved by Judge Dee, a famous magistrate active during the T'ang dynasty.

Van Gulik's subtle way of teaching was most helpful to me—he really does explain what goes on. Zen Buddhism being around in ancient China, as in present day Japan—Dee not being a Buddhist but a Confucianist with an open mind—Confucianism and Buddhism not as opposed as I thought, and Taoism intertwining the two within the Far Eastern mind—all this I saw clearly in van Gulik's *oeuvre,* and his probings helped me understand where my own adventures led me.

How did the erudite sinologue take to his new role as a popular thriller writer?

He liked it; he saw himself as a practising artist. He wanted to be accepted by his colleagues. Ab Visser, an untranslated Dutch author at the time, told me later that van Gulik both intimidated and irritated him. Van Gulik,

*1958

on leave in The Netherlands, or temporarily residing in
his own country, always looked Visser up and insisted on
an easy friendship. "An *ambassador*," Visser told me.
"Can you imagine? Chap in a *limo* with a uniformed driver
up front. The man spoke *Chinese*. A crazy fellow. He'd
take me to these restaurants." Most Dutchmen eat Chinese food but van Gulik took his literary friend to elite
establishments where he would have the owner come to
the table to discuss the menu in Mandarin. Visser knew
about fried rice and fried noodles, maybe with some veg-
gies on top, but there was glazed and baked duck, too,
that would fall apart into a three-dimensional jigsaw
puzzle, crablegs caught in an obscure river, and Chinese
eighty-proof 'wines' that tore the skin off his palate. "And
expensive," Visser said. "We would eat all my royalties
for a year, for I wouldn't let him pay, just to show him, of
course."

Another Dutch author of detective novels, Pim Hof-
dorp, merely shrugged when I asked him about his friend
van Gulik. He showed me a rare first edition of *Dee
Goong An*, that van Gulik translated from Chinese into
English and which he had privately printed in Japan just
after the war. When I went "Ah" and "Oh"—for I hadn't
seen the book since I had read it furtively in the holy
room at Daitoku-ji, the Zen temple in Kyoto—Pim gave it
to me and wished me luck. "You've read it?" I asked. He
nodded. "Sure. Chinesey, you know. Bit out of the way." It
had been a present from long ago. Van Gulik had died
meanwhile and Pim was going too. He thought the book
would do well on my shelf, where it has been through
today.

Pride is a strange vice and has a hold on all of us. Van
Gulik wanted to be an accepted novelist. He had few lit-

erary friends, his Dutch publisher, van Hoeve, hardly ever answered a letter and didn't believe in praise, and the Dutch critics were mostly shortsighted and unkind. The public liked him though, and he received some fan-mail, mostly from women, as he told a reporter once. The ladies fancied Judge Dee and wanted him to engage in a little 'hankiepankie.' Van Gulik, although eager to please, couldn't bring the exclusive magistrate down to such a low level, but he did include erotic scenes in later books, reserving the male parts for Dee's lieutenants. I kept asking people who knew van Gulik what he had been like. The response was modest, and pointed at opposites that couldn't harmonize too well. Jolly, and aloof. Calm, sometimes irritable. At peace, and driven by unrelenting forces. Detached, and saddened by human ignorance.

A retired consul told me how he was having a good time in Japan when Head Office The Hague suddenly transferred him to South Korea. He didn't like Korea. He disliked it so much that he began to sicken. He wrote to his former chief, Ambassador van Gulik, pleading for a return to Japan. The letter was forwarded from Tokyo to The Hague, where van Gulik had meanwhile been hospitalized, for what turned out to be a terminal lung affliction. Van Gulik, only 57, always smoked—cigars, cigarettes, pipes, anything he could put his hands on. He'd been warned many times, for his sharp chronic cough was correctly diagnosed as a cancer symptom. Now, too late to change his ways, he smoked cigars in the hospital's private room while his condition rapidly wors-ened. The consul from Korea, on leave in The Hague, vis-ited him, without mentioning his possible transfer. "Right," van Gulik, who remembered the letter, said. "Hand me that telephone." It was the ambassador's last call, but the consul could go back to his beloved Japan. "Don't you mind dying, sir?" the consul asked. "Forgive me a little lofty talk," van Gulik said, "but all movement is illusory. From Seoul to Kobe. From life to death."

John Blofeld, a British sinologist and Buddhist, who spent many years in China and now lives in Bangkok, knew van Gulik from the time that they both served as diplomats in Chungking, during WW II. I asked him to pass on some of his personal impressions. Blofeld patted my shoulder for admiring van Gulik "because his example is most helpful in smoothing the path of the less gifted and marginally advanced." He described my hero as a large cheerful man who used the same Dutch accent in Italian as in Sanskrit. Part of Blofeld's letter, written in red ink, I had to promise not to quote, which is a pity. I will quote some of the rest later on in this attempted treatise.

Van Gulik liked cartoons, part of the trivial media he followed. Had he lived longer he might have tried movie scripts, for he enjoyed "envisaging a story in pictures." A number of his tales were adapted for cartoons and he trained a Dutch draftsman, Frits Kroezeman, to take care of proper Chinese-style illustrations. The strips, not easily available in English to my knowledge, eventually filled eight volumes after being serialized in several Dutch papers. Mr. Kroezeman, who spent many hours at van Gulik's bedside, told me that "Robert wasn't in the least frightened of death. He accepted his approaching disappearance most stoically. A most courageous man indeed!"

Although never engaged in any type of combat, van Gulik had faced death many times before. The second world war found him in Tokyo, where, several months after hostilities were declared, he was, as a diplomat, allowed to evacuate to China. The temporary Chinese capital was then Chungking, hit daily by fierce Japanese bombing. Van Gulik, having lost all his clothes in a fire, calmly wandered about in Chinese garb, holding onto a satchel of books that he happened to be reading. Some weeks later, when all diplomats were spending most of their time in underground shelters, he was complaining about dust that interfered with his calligraphy. Still later he started work on a dissertation describing various ways in which the Chinese and Japanese mount scrolls, and he would rush about in between bombings to collect paper samples in the artists' stores of the town.

Years later, when stationed in Beirut, revolution broke out and van Gulik had his family shipped back to The Hague. Alone behind sandbags he worked on one of his Judge Dees. "It's a bit awkward," he wrote to a friend, "for it is hard to concentrate when Arabs keep dropping dynamite sticks in my garden. So far I have managed to throw them all back."

The Mugar Memorial Library at Boston University keeps four blue carton boxes that contain manuscripts and notes van Gulik sent them before his death. I dived straight into them, looking for the secret of his living diligence and peaceful death. Although the experts assure us that van Gulik bypassed the essential disciplines of religion and philosophy, I would suggest that he did, in fact, practise the more esoteric Taoist and Buddhist instructions. Both Taoism and Zen claim to have empty cores that, once touched by the adept, give access to the secret art of doing nothing, *wu-wei*. Not 'doing nothing' in the sense of shirking one's duty, as Carl Jung explains, but rather the practice of 'quiet acceptance of that which happens to us so that we can happen along.' Van Gulik himself called the technique 'being engaged in nothing.' Chuang-tzu (end of the fourth century B.C.) wrote a poem on the subject, and one of the Mugar-kept carton boxes holds van Gulik's translation:

You can't say Tao exists,
You can't say Tao does not exist,
But you can find it in the silence,
in wu-wei *(deedlessness).*

Dr. Robert Hans van Gulik died in The Hague, 1967, and was born in another Dutch town, provincial Zutphen, 1910.

1910 was a quiet year, before the wars, when God still ruled in heaven and all was well below. Dutch society was sorted in neat boxes and the van Guliks were up top, for Dr. van Gulik, Sr., was a high medical officer with the Dutch Colonial Army, Dutch Indies. The Indies, of course, were happy to be ruled by white men abroad and their main purpose was to provide their enlightened rulers with an abundance of useful products. Father van Gulik was stationed in Holland when Robert was born, and the family returned to the Far East when the boy was three years old. He lived in Java (first in Surabaya, later in Batavia—now Djakarta) until he was twelve. At elementary school he was taught Dutch only, while most people around him spoke Malay, Javanese or Chinese. Having a good ear he picked up a number of words while learning their meanings, but he also wanted to be able to read and write. As he found the Chinese signs on storefronts fascinating he had the owners explain them. Soon he was

scratching the intricate characters in the sand of un-
paved streets and passerby stopped to see what the little
boy was doing. Chinese storekeepers showed him how
each character is built up from a limited number of parts,
and the eager student soon saw how seemingly endless
combinations originate in common ground. Compared to
Chinese, Malay and Javanese were easy enough, and he
absorbed the languages as he wandered about. Being a
natural collector he noted words in separate exercise
books, decorating the pages with his own illustrations.
When the family returned to Holland in 1922 Robert was
fairly fluent in four languages, and ready, at twelve, to
enter high school. High school, in his case, naturally
meant 'gymnasium,' where Greek and Latin are taught
along with French, German and English, with advanced
mathematics, physics and chemistry thrown in, too. After
Chinese none of the languages seemed difficult in any
way. By happy chance the boy met Holland's most cele-
brated linguist, C. C. Uhlenbeck, who recognized van Gulik's gifts and taught him Russian, and when there was
still room, Sanskrit as well. The professor was working
on a dictionary of the Blackfoot Indian language and van
Gulik joined him, resulting in publication a few years
later. Van Gulik's first love, Chinese, had not been forgotten, but wasn't taught anywhere near Nymegen, the city
where the family was living then. He advertised and a
Chinese student of agriculture responded. The teacher
was paid out of van Gulik's pocket money, which meant
Robert had to go short on luxuries that other boys his age
enjoyed as a matter of course.

At that time he began to publish in the school's
monthly paper, *Rostra*. His poetry was popular with the
other students, and an essay called "From the Beautiful

Isle" made a definite impression on students and teachers alike. Van Gulik was only eighteen then, but his style was both pleasing and sincere. He remembers his visits as a child to the Chinese quarter of Batavia:

The small room is only illuminated by faint paper lanterns, hung from solid smoke-blackened beams, supporting a ceiling that slopes by the weight of many floors above. The dim light makes space and furnishings look picturesque: in a corner I see shelves bearing heavy loads of Chinese books. Further along the wall is the home altar, framed by glowing red cloth, on which some succinct and beautiful saying of K'ung Fu-tzu is written. There is also a low table on which a delicate porcelain bowl is placed. A small charcoal stove glows in the room's center, warming the old watchman who has stretched himself on the couch, comfortable in his white cotton suit with wide sleeves and trouser-legs: small squinting eyes recessed between hundreds of wrinkles in his kindly shriveled face. He cheerfully greets me and says, in the rounded tones of Kwantung-Chinese, that the noodles are done. But I prefer to climb the rickety stairs and reach the tower that offers a splendid view of the Chinese town ... a sea of roofs, randomly placed just everywhere, showing up like choppy waves in a wonderfully wild sea.

He wanted to go back to those happy days of his youth and quotes the poet Li Po (701–762) who, under similar circumstances, sighs: "I lower my head and think of my country." There's still a long wait but, fortunately, much to do. He is accepted at the famous University of Leyden where he studies Oriental Languages, and begins to publish immediately, most unusual for a mere pupil. His

learned articles, clever essays and meticulous transla-
tions draw attention. In 1932, three years before his doctorate, he publishes the Dutch version of a play written
by the Indian Kàlidása in Sanskrit (400 B.C.). At 24 he
has his master's degree and a year later, at Utrecht University, his Ph.D., *cum laude,* on a thesis entitled *Adora-
tion of the Horse in China, Japan, India and Tibet.* Brill
of Leyden, publishers of scholastic material, are surprised
when the booklet goes through a number of reprints.
Only 25 years old, Robert van Gulik presents himself as
an established scholar.

Now what? Work? He could perhaps have stayed and
lectured but the Orient waited, far beyond the tiny fron-
tiers of The Netherlands. Traditionally the male van Guliks were military men ("All the adults around," van
Gulik would say, "seem to belong to the species 'sabretiger' "). Perhaps his linguistic reputation might impress
the Foreign Service? He applied and became a secretary
at the legation in Tokyo, in 1935, where nothing but very
slow advancement (and a great deal of free time) could
be expected. Van Gulik fitted in well for he liked being
a 'gentlemen of scholastic habits.' As a schoolboy he had
written, on the subject of Chinese reforms: *"From a practical point of view this is better* [than the old school sys-
tem]. *All these changes are in the natural course of things,
and they are very good. But unconsciously one starts to
wonder whether among all those modern people the old-
fashioned fine type* of literatus *will continue to exist, of
the kind we had to mourn recently when the old states-
man/author Ku Hung-ming died—he, who had not been
afraid to cling calmly to the old 'Religion of the Gentleman,' at a time when all kinds of new ideas were pouring
into China from all sides. Of course there are advantages*

and disadvantages in everything, and we, contemporaries, cannot determine whether these have to be considered as improvements, or not. This is a task for those who come after us." (Elseviers Magazine LXXXVII, page 320)

The next seven years gave him ample opportunities to be the "Western mandarin," the studious aristocrat, the serious scholar who looks into sideways, little alleys of thought and art that are not usually investigated by the sweeping spirits of the time. Van Gulik studies Chinese and Japanese criminal law, the art of bookprinting and mounting scrolls, plays the Chinese lute and reads up on music composed for this instrument; he peruses (in a 'desultory fashion,' he modestly claims) medicine and crime detection, and starts an art collection that will be lost at least twice, and eventually fetch a fortune at Christies' Amsterdam auction of December 7, 1983.

A Chinese gentleman who knew him smiled when he remembered the dark-eyed blond-haired giant whose mind and bearing, he assured, me, were typically Chinese. "An incarnation, no doubt," he mused, "of an illustrious spirit from our far past, choosing to come back to us with a sense of humor." Van Gulik was, by his learned colleagues, given a Chinese name based on the sounds of his name, *Kao Lo-pei*, 高 羅 佩, (*Kao* = Gu, *Lo-pei* = Robert), a name that was signed proudly under his dissertations in Chinese. As the 'honorable Kao' he would be accepted as a true Chinese scholar in the many countries where he lived from then on.

His Chinese studies, so pleasurably continued in Tokyo, were followed by even more intense dedication in China proper when he was evacuated to Chungking in 1942, together with all the other diplomats of countries then at war with Japan. Van Gulik was happy there, and didn't want to leave, but the war ended and The Hague called him back. Rather than be unhappy he resumed his studies at Leyden University. A transfer to Washington followed, where he could make use of the American libraries and meet eminent sinologues, but he preferred the Far East and was pleased when he could return to Tokyo in 1949. He left in 1953 and was sent to New Delhi, Kuala Lumpur and later the Lebanon—each transfer involving a considerable promotion. In Beirut he became Dutch foreign minister for the Middle East. Finally, in 1965, he was appointed Dutch ambassador to Japan, a post he held until his death a mere two years later. Only change is constant; not even pain lasts. He had realized that truth before, when he translated a Japanese poem:

Washi ga shinotote (When I shall die)

When I shall die
Who will remember me in sorrow?
Only the black mountain crows
will visit my grave.
But the crows that fly from the mountain top
will not feel any sorrow either:
Except for the funeral cookies that they can't reach
Placed on an altar that celebrates my death.

3

Van Gulik was not well known as a sinologue except within university circles, until the rebirth of Judge Dee, of course. Before Dee few of his publications managed to reach the general public. *Sexual Life in Ancient China,* published by E. J. Brill (Leyden University Press) in 1961, was a fat tome of over 400 pages, attractively bound but too scientific and pricy to appeal to the layman. The same goes for another, even more scholarly and voluminous volume, *Chinese Pictorial Art,* published (1958) by the *Estituto Italiano per Il Medio ed Estremo Oriente* in Rome. Then there was *The Gibbon in China (An Essay in Chinese Animal Lore),* published by Brill again, in 1967, and even more obscure booklets such as *Hsi K'ang and his Poetical Essay on the Lute* (Tokyo, Sophia University, 1941). His privately printed pamphlets such as *Book Illustration During the Ming Dynasty* (in Dutch) were printed in very limited editions, meant to be given away to friends and relations. Some copies found their way at cost to 'chinoiserie' bookshops and stores but none was ever set up to be commercially successful.

Original woodblock print cover done by van Gulik for
his 1949 translation of *Dee Goong An*

All this changed when van Gulik translated and published *Dee Goong An*.

A mandarin, a Chinese literary gentleman, never deigned to mention his own name, unless he wrote educative works or historical tales, forms of literature that were approved by the Imperial Court. A pen name had to cover up any attempts at fiction. An author who 'made up' was no artist but an artisan; his status was about as low as that of an actor or streetsinger, even if the public loved everything he did. That's why nobody knows who wrote *Dee Goong An* (Criminal Cases Solved by Judge Dee). The book appeared in the eighteenth century, and was a true whodunit, preceding the genre in the West. Van Gulik found his first copy in 1940. Enthused by its fascinating plots (Judge Dee solves three unrelated cases) van Gulik made enquiries and found that the book had been in print for hundreds of years. It would be the foundation for his own lengthy series, but he didn't know that as he ran about, gathering information on the historical judge (630–700) Ti Jen-chieh, who started his career as magistrate and finished as a minister of state. As a novel the book was great but it had also considerable value as a historical source, supplying more information about the (in)famous dynasty of Tang.

Van Gulik immediately began to do an English translation and passed the manuscript (1949) to his acquaintances in Japan. Everyone showed enthusiasm so he risked a private printing of 1200 copies, 'bound in an original wood print and signed and sealed by the author.' The edition sold out (I suspect he gave a good number away) and was reprinted (1975) by Dover Publications in New York.

The character "Judge Dee" made a deep impression on van Gulik. Being an aficionado of the detective genre he corresponded with several American and British authors, whom he sent copies of *Dee Goong An*, suggesting that they would come up with fresh plots. The writers, knowing their limitations, bowed out. He tired to realize the idea himself and wrote *The Chinese Bell* and *The Chinese Maze Murders* (1950) in English. The latter was published at once in Japan and sold easily, because, unkind critics claimed, he had insisted that there would be a naked lady (drawn by his own hand) on the cover. His subsequent Chinese version did equally well, titled *Ti Jen-chieh Ch'i-an* (Singapore, 1953). Van Gulik's effort was idealistic. He was appalled by merely sensational or pornographic trash appearing in the bookstalls of the Orient, and meant to reacquaint the public with the very best of its own values, as embodied in the core of the Ancient Chinese Empire. Michael Joseph of London printed van Gulik's English manuscript, an immediate bestseller (1953). Van Gulik was on his way as a popular and exotic thriller writer and became famous, especially in the English speaking world, where the reading public had been exposed to whodunits since the inimitable Sherlock Holmes. Van Gulik's creation was a welcome nouveauté. The number of British and American editions of a series that would, ultimately, comprise sixteen volumes, was astounding—all volumes were recently reprinted again by Scribners and the University of Chicago Press, and many covers show erotic designs drawn by the author. The sexual aspect has undoubtedly added to the series' success, and is historically acceptable, for the T'ang Chinese were openly sensuous. Each book contains several stimulating scenes, which are always illustrated by van Gulik, not in the T'ang style but in keeping with the Ming tradition—simple line figures that guide the reader's imagination.

◊ ◊ ◊

Ab Visser, the Dutch crime author cultivated by van
Gulik, told me that his famous friend, after some sips of
jenever, would whisper: "Judge Dee is me." Not really too
surprising. Conan Doyle was Sherlock Holmes, Chandler
Marlowe, Hammett Sam Spade. An author will project
himself; who else can he push on his stage? Even when
he does try to create others he can only shape from that
part of his character that is either observable or hides itself in a shadow. In order to form a *hero* certain parts of
the self are combined optimally, and we see the author as
he would like to see himself. Often, even if the writer
does his best, he comes up with a caricature, like Tin Tin,
James Bond, Charlie Chan, even Holmes. Exceptionally,
van Gulik presents us with a true hero, the ideal father
figure (who, in order not to bore the kids, will interrupt
his loving admonitions with splendid swordplay and
feats of spectacular and superior cunning), even a potential and most desirable lover (wide chested, tall, athletic
and intellectual, the reading ladies could never make a
better choice), who knows how to behave. So that we may
have an even more complete image van Gulik sometimes
describes his and our hero's dreams.

Now why all this? Is there a connection? Methinks
there is. Dee came from a nice family—his father was a
high official in the capital—and never had to face the
dreary trouble that confronted a less lucky fellow whose
house didn't view the river but the swamp. It was to be
expected that Dee would pass the examinations set by
the state, but he did more than that, he broke through
the limitations applied to his kind. Like van Gulik, scion

of a tribe of 'sabretigers,' destined to enjoy a flashing career, Dee was more than the standard product of his type—the man was definitely a genius. Like van Gulik Dee specialized in following sidestreets and alleys, rather than strolling down easy boulevards. He studied law rather than philosophy, medicine rather than poetic accounts of mythical ancient lives. Like van Gulik again Dee spoke another dialect, for we hear him hold forth in Cantonese, a language entirely different from Mandarin, even if it uses the same script. Dee's profession of magistrate equals that of an ambassador and Dee was eventually promoted to minister of state and counsellor at the court of the terrible Empress Wu, a crazy lady whose disastrous power games he learned to control, without losing his own head. Whoever glances at the history of the T'ang dynasty will agree that only a Superior Man could cope with such horrible and sadistic bloodshed. Dee was straight. Van Gulik must have been incorruptible too, but Dee made more contact with the people's souls than van Gulik ever could, for Dee, today, is an archetype who survived even the Cultural Revolution, and can be seen all over the most populous nation on earth, stamping on platforms in his brocade robes.

That van Gulik likes to identify with Dee will have other reasons. The Judge is a handsome wide-shouldered giant with a full flowing beard. He is a master sword- and stickfighter and advanced in the art of Chinese boxing—the prototype of both judo and karate. He is also courageous and likes to mix, incognito under a variety of guises, among the common folks. These superman aspects were beyond van Gulik to assume, given the time and the places reserved for his own life, but in some details he could certainly resemble his superior ego. There are the bizarre

details of both van Gulik and Dee consorting with gibbons, and both playing the Chinese lute.

A clever author knows how to put his hero down, for
only holy men never stumble and fall, and infallible
holiebolies are no longer *en vogue*. Modern man has
learned how to be cynical and too many con-gurus have
spoiled their market. Readers, like authors, like to identify with the hero, but they can only *be* Dee if the judge
loses a few too. Dee, therefore, is introduced to us with
the negative trait of arrogance, as in real life perhaps too,
because Chinese, and especially those from up high, could
and can be quite conceited. China in Chinese is still 'The
Middle Country,' and whatever isn't China has been
pushed to the sides. Non-Chinese, and van Gulik always
manages to introduce a few into each tale, were inferiors
to Dee and he kept shaking his sleeves angrily when they
dared to accost him. He addresses them *briefly*. "Have
you noticed," a friend wrote to me once, "how often Judge
Dee addresses inferiors *briefly*?" He is right, but we don't
have to see Dee as a grouchy chauvinist either. He always bothers to find out what the foreigners want and
has been known to secretly admire some of their creations.
The negative side is understated, however, for Dee is a
just official, accessible to laborers at the minimum wage,
beggars, even women, and will defend their cases if he
feels they have been wronged. Dee will not desist until
the victims' wounds have been healed and the downtrod-
den can rise and be respected as citizens of their mighty
country, as restored individuals, who can once more contribute to the common valor.

Other nouveautés were added by van Gulik, that
helped sell his books to the proper public. Readers of
whodunits were used to one detective solving one crime

in one book, and it hadn't occurred to them yet that such a situation could be most unreal. This is a bad *bad* world and evil strikes simultaneously in many places. Even private eyes, if they are good (and who wants to read about the offside of the profession?) are kept busy by many clients at the same time. Dee was a magistrate in ancient China. The position entailed more than simply being judge—he was also a police chief, city manager and number one tax collector. Criminals thumbed their noses and didn't wait for one crime to be solved before they committed more dastardly deeds. Because of this most of the van Gulik thrillers contain more than one plot, so poor Dee is sent rushing from one location to another, and hardly has time for any homelife that, however, when he does get a chance to be entertained by his four charming wives, gets into the books too.

Van Gulik dropped his scholarly mask when he wrote the Dee saga, and not all of the facts related can be historically proved.

In order to provide a backbone of reference for his readers he wrote down his fictitious version of the magistrate's life.*

---

*Fictitious, except for his birthdate, and the historical note at the end, and covering 14 novels and 8 short stories. (Taken from the Scribner edition of *Judge Dee at Work*, the chronology does not include the events of *Necklace and Calabash* [1966] and *Poets and Murder* [1967]).

Time, place and Judge Dee's office	Titles (the short stories in *Judge Dee at Work* are marked by an asterisk)	Information on Judge Dee, his family, his lieutenants, and persons who appear in more than one story (page numbers refer to the first English editions)
A.D. 630 Tai-yuan, capital of Shansi Province.		Judge Dee born. Receives elementary education at home. Passes the provincial literary examinations.
650 The capital.		Judge Dee's father appointed Imperial Councillor in the capital. Judge Dee acts as his father's private secretary, marries his First and Second Ladies. Passes metropolitan literary examination, and is appointed secretary in the Imperial Archives.
663 Magistrate of Peng-lai, a district on the northeast coast of the Chinese-Empire.	*The Chinese Gold Murders* (London, 1959). The Murdered Magistrate. The Bolting Bride, The Butchered Bully.	Judge Dee's first independent official post. Proceeds there accompanied by Sergeant Hoong. Meets on the way Ma Joong and Chiao Tai. First mention of the sword Rain Dragon; Chiao Tai foresees he will be killed by that sword (p. 31). Ch. XV describes adventures of Miss Tsao.
	Five Auspicious Clouds	One week after Judge Dee's arrival in Peng-lai. Mrs. Ho: suicide or murder? Solved by Judge Dee alone.
	The Red Tape Murder	One month later. A military murder, solved by Judge Dee, assisted by Ma Joong and Chiao Tai. Colonel Meng appears.
	He Came with the Rain	Six months later. Murder of a pawnbroker, solved by Judge Dee alone. Colonel Meng is again referred to. Judge Dee decides to marry Miss Tsao as his Third Lady.

663	*The Lacquer Screen* (London, 1962). The Lacquer Screen, The Credulous Merchant, The Faked Accounts.	Solved by Judge Dee, assisted by Chiao Tai, during a brief sojourn in the district Wei-ping. Second reference to Chiao Tai dying by the sword (p. 140).
666 Magistrate of Hanyuan, a district on the bank of a lake, near the capital.	*The Chinese Lake Murders* (London, 1960). The Drowned Courtesan, The Vanished Bride, The Spendthrift Councillor.	Solved by Judge Dee, Hoong, Ma Joong and Chiao Tai. His future fourth lieutenant Tao Gan here makes his first appearance (p. 153). The rich landowner Han Yung-han appears (*passim*). Description of the King of the Beggars of Han-yuan (p. 118).
	The Morning of the Monkey (in *The Monkey and the Tiger* [London, 1965]).	Murder of a tramp, solved by Judge Dee and Tao Gan; Tao Gan is definitely taken into Judge Dee's service. The King of the Beggars reappears (p. 31). Han Yung-han mentioned (p. 59).
	The Haunted Monastery (London, 1961). The Embalmed Abbot, The Pious Maid, The Morose Monk. **The Murder on the Lotus Pond*	Scene is laid in an old Taoist temple, in the mountains of Han-yuan. Murders solved by Judge Dee, with Tao Gan. Judge Dee's attitude to his wives described on p. 12. The murder of an old poet, solved by Judge Dee, with Ma Joong.
668 Magistrate of Poo-yang, a large, flourishing district in Kiangsu Province, on the Grand Canal.	*The Chinese Bell Murders* (London, 1958). The Rape Murder in Half Moon Street, The Secret of the Buddhist Temple, The Mysterious Skeleton.	Solved by Judge Dee, with his four lieutenants Sergeant Hoong, Ma Joong, Chiao Tai and Tao Gan. Introduction of Sheng Pa, Head of the Beggars (*passim*). Introduction of Magistrate Lo, of the neighboring district (Ch. IX).
	*The Two Beggars	Murder solved by Judge Dee, with Sergeant Hoong. Magistrate Lo referred to again.

The Wrong Sword

Murder of a young acrobat, solved by Judge Dee, with Ma Joong and Chiao Tai. Sheng Pa reappears.

The Red pavilion (London, 1964). The Callous Courtesan, The Amorous Academician, The Unlucky Lovers.

Scene is laid in the amusement resort of Paradise Island where Judge Dee stays two days with Ma Joong. Magistrate Lo reappears in Chapters II and XX.

The Emperor's Pearl (London, 1963). The Dead Drummer, The Murdered Slavemaid, the Emperor's Pearl.

Murders during the annual boat races, solved by Judge Dee, assisted by Sergeant Hoong. Sheng Pa reappears in ChapterVIII; his romance with Miss Violet Liang.

670
Magistrate of Lan-fang, a district on the extreme western frontier.

The Chinese Maze Murders (London, 1952). The Murder in the Sealed Room, The Hidden Testament, The Girl with the Severed Head.

On p. 22 are given the reasons for Judge Dee's abrupt transfer to this remote border district. The overthrow of a local tyrant and several mysterious murders, solved by Judge Dee, with Hoong, Ma Joong, Chiao Tai and Tao Gan. The Uigur girl Tulbee becomes Ma Joong's sweetheart (p. 173). Headman Fang's story (p. 35); Fang's son appointed constable (p. 289).

The Phantom of the Temple (London, 1966).

Three crimes that turn out to be one, solved by Judge Dee with Sergeant Hoong and Ma Joong. Description of Judge Dee's three wives on p. 40; more details about his Third Lady (the former Miss Tsao) on p. 104. The Uigur girl Tulbee reappears (p. 56). References to Headman Fang and his son (pp. 11 and 136).

The Coffins of the Emperor

Two difficult cases solved by Judge Dee alone, when summoned to the border district Ta-shih-kou during the Tar-tar war.

Murder on New Year's Eve

A most unusual case, solved by Judge Dee alone, after he had been four years in Lan-fang.

676 Magistrate of Pei-chow, a desolate district up in the barren north.	*The Chinese Nail Murders* (London, 1961). The Headless Corpse, The Paper Cat, The Murdered Merchant.	After only a few months in this new post, Judge Dee was appointed Lord Chief Justice, in the capital. In Pei-chow he solves several particularly cruel murders, with Sergeant Hoong, Ma Joong, Chiao Tai and Tao Gan; but Sergeant Hoong is killed while working on a case. The antecedents of Judge Dee's three wives are given on p. 116. Introduction of Mrs. Kuo, the Lady of the Medicine Hill (p. 38).
	The Night of the Tiger (in *The Monkey and the Tiger* [London, 1965]).	Murder of a young girl solved by Judge Dee alone when, on his way from pei-chow to the capital, he has to stay overnight in a lonely country house. References to Mrs. Kuo and Sergeant Hoong's death, on p. 91.
677 Lord Chief Justice, in the Imperial Capital.	*The Willow Pattern* (London, 1965). The Willow Pattern, The Steep Staircase, The Murdered Bondmaid.	Judge Dee has taken up his new office of Lord Chief Justice. Ma Joong and Chiao Tai have been appointed Colonels of the Guard, Tao Gan chief secretary of the Metropolitan Court. Ma Joong marries the Yuan twin sisters.
681 Lord Chief Justice.	*Murder in Canton* (London, 1966). The Vanished Censor, The Smaragdine Dancer, The Golden Bell.	Scene is laid in Canton, where Judge Dee has been sent on a special mission. Murders solves by Judge Dee, with the assistance of Chiao Tai and Tao Gan. Chiao Tai is killed by the sword Rain Dragon. Tao Gan decides to marry Miss Liang. Reference to Mrs. Kuo and the tragedy on Medicine Hill on p. 160.

Historical Note. Judge Dee died in A.D. 700, at the age of seventy. He was survived by two sons, Dee Guang-se and Dee Djing-hui, who had honorable official careers without, however, particularly distinguishing themselves. It was his grandson Dee Djien-mo who inherited his grandfather's remarkable personality and great wisdom; he died as governor of the Imperial Capital.

4

Prophets are proverbially unpopular at home, and there seemed to be a conspiracy of Dutch reviewers reviling the Judge Dee books when they first came out in the late fifties and early sixties. Maybe there was jealousy, one of the rotten pillars on which any human society totters. The series was definitely a sensation and sales were good, but the knowledgeable gentlemen who judge books for a living may have envied a successful new novelist who already was a top diplomat and a published scholar, and could, perhaps, have tried to keep him out of 'their' market. Whatever the unpleasant reason, they all jumped on van Gulik with their boots on. Negative comments were usually in the same vein: "Robert van Gulik's books, in spite of their success both in the Orient and the West, can by their very nature on no account be considered to have literary value," and "the success of these cheap 'exotic' thrillers must be due solely to the modern affliction of wanting to vicariously enjoy gore and low lust, rather than wishing to learn about another civilization." Nowhere did anyone official accept the author's erudition. When his publisher, van Hoeve, died and van Gulik himself also departed, the series was allowed to slip away. Another house bought van Hoeve's business but did not bother about Judge Dee, and I was asked (1978) to help some fans to have the series reprinted. Our best argument were the skyhigh prices that first editions of his work commanded, and some recent foreign editions that I could show around. The new publisher listened and sold nearly a million copies within the next five years. Van Gulik's memory might have smiled at this glorious second wave of fame, although both his training and his studies would have lifted his susceptibility high above mere human judgment. In the Mugar Library boxes I found another Japanese poem that could have expressed his feelings:

Seki no yugiri (Evening Fog on the Mountain Pass)

Does the temple bell ring?
Or is this the sound of its clapper?
The sound has to come from somewhere
between bell and clapper.

There's a Dutch saying: "To hear the bell toll without knowing where the clapper hangs." Van Gulik may have thought of the proverb when he translated the little poem, expressing human ignorance. It isn't hard to imagine the heavyset Dutchman—ambassador, sinologist, mandarin, art collector, popular novelist—wandering through the fog on some oriental mountain pass, wondering about human effort and relativity, feeling both free and lost in his self appreciation and with the ideas of others.

His friend John Blofeld, the British official who shared his Chungking war experiences, gained a reputation as a mystic, a Buddhist adept. Blofeld, like van Gulik, spoke, wrote and read Chinese fluently. Blofeld, who now lives in Bangkok, known to me by his many books on Buddhist and Taoist enlightenment, all gentle studies of lofty subjects, was kind enough to answer my letter requesting to "please pass me any details that you may remember from your encounters with Dr. van Gulik." He permitted me to quote his comments, dated 8 May 1978:

"I knew Robert rather well and saw him often from 1943 to 1945, for I was then Cultural Attaché to the British Embassy, Chungking, and he was a secretary or had some fairly senior position in the Netherlands Legation. We were drawn together by our mutual interests in things Chinese; though as far as I know, he remained always a scholar pure and simple in the sense that his interest in Chinese religions, unlike mine, did not extend to having any religious beliefs or taking more than a scholar's and artist's interest in them. Even in those days, his room was more like the study of a Chinese literatus than a diplomat's. A big man with a great zest for life and ready laughter, he resembled an Elizabethan statesman in many ways, if one can imagine such a person with a background of Eastern rather than Renaissance culture. For all that he was a truly wonderful linguist, he never lost his strong Dutch accent in either English or Chinese. Everybody liked him and it was something of a privilege to be singled out as a friend by such a man.

"He was not married until towards the end of that period, but at some time or other became engaged to his future wife, a Miss Sui from Peking. I liked her very much,

**The marriage of Shui Shifang and Robert van Gulik;
Chungking, 1943**

*but did not know her well as he was still a bachelor for
most of my time in Chungking. I imagine she must have
been a girl with a rather old-fashioned Chinese scholarly
background (unusual in that time and place) for her to
have attracted him.*

*"At that time, Robert could do four astonishing things,
any one of which would have been extraordinary in a Western man. He could write Chinese 'grass' (running) characters well enough for his Chinese friends to appreciate his
wall scrolls of running calligraphy; he could play the classical Chinese lute (ku ch'in) with seven silken strings; he
could write books in Chinese for Chinese readers; and he
could cut good Chinese seals on hard stone! Later, I discovered that he was also excellent in Sanskrit, Malay and,
above all, Japanese, as well as being fluent in several Western languages and knowing Latin well. In spite of being a
diplomat and good at his job, he found time (after his
Chungking days) to write his extraordinary books, such as
one on two hundred kinds of paper used for mounting
Japanese scrolls, another on a certain kind of bamboo
flute, a very scholarly book on sex-life in ancient China,
and—just for fun—the Judge Dee books. What a man!*

*"Between 1951 when I arrived in Bangkok and his
death in 1967, he came to Bangkok several times and we
had joyful reunions, but so brief that they provided no material for me to add to what I have said already, except for
one incident. While visiting the Buddha-room in my house,
he pointed to the* dorjeh *(Vajra)* and the* dorjeh-*topped*

---

*A *dorjeh* is a, usually elaborate, decorated little stick-like object that Tibetan Buddhist high priests (ranking as *lamas*)
carry and manipulate as a sign of their rank: the decorations
consist of two stylized ornaments.

*bell which, to Tibetans, symbolize many pairs of opposites
that need to be unified, but especially Means (compassion)
and Goal (wisdom), and explained to me what he called
their sexual origin as representatives of the male and female organs. Well, I just smiled and said nothing much. Of
course in a certain way he was not wrong, but his assertion
was a gross over-simplification quite surprising in so great
a scholar. From this and some other things, I gathered
that, despite his amazing linguistic skills, his passion for
study and his profound appreciation of the arts, he was
never attracted (as some more recent scientists and scholars have been) by the* numinous *components of Chinese
and Indian religions. Whether C. G. Jung recognized these
but avoided saying too much in his published works for
fear of harming his reputation as a scholar, Robert, I
think, was completely blind to this particular aspect of
Eastern studies. If I am right, it is not to his discredit and
not at all surprising; because it is only very recently that
learned Western scholars have begun to allow the possibility that these numinous elements really do exist. Most
scholars of his day and age would have laughed at them
as, I think, Robert did—the result of the rigid beliefs then
current in scholastic circles. One cannot image him keeping the* I Ching *reverently wrapped in fine cloth, unless for
the sake of the cloth's beauty or as a friendly gesture to his
Chinese friends. I think one could describe him as an extroverted man. Yours sincerely, John Blofeld . . ."*

Devout mystic versus cynical scholar. Perhaps. Good
friends, once separated, travel different roads and may
end up in very dissimilar locations. Van Gulik may not
have burned incense in his study to please Buddhist stat-

ues, and he may have shied away from the esoteric practice of long daily hours of motionless meditation, but it
seems to me that Blofeld grossly underestimates his
learned friend's profound insights. Van Gulik certainly
avoided the mystic trap that changes the sincerely curious into sternfaced holy men shuffling about in a fog of
self satisfaction, but his heroes, both Judge Dee, and Me-
neer Hendricks whom we'll meet in his only 'Dutch' novel
(*The Given Day*) are interesting projections of van Gulik's
own human quest. Perhaps I can show some proof that
may contradict Mr. Blofeld's too negative suspicions.

Van Gulik in the library of his Tokyo residence, 1948

5

Van Gulik never wrote a survey of the three Chinese religions (Confucianism, Taoism and Buddhism), not, like John Blofeld suggests, because he had no knowledge of the 'central issues,' but rather, I would think, because he was too intelligent to express himself in clear language on subjects that, by their very nature, tend to slip away from our grasp. The essential secret that realizes itself at any moment in a limitless creation can't be caught in mere words and the sage's modesty makes him put down his pen. The secret, nevertheless, does have a way of wafting itself through all human games and it would be egocentrical, and perhaps even silly, to stay completely quiet once we have gained some insight at all. The light, the holy men say, has to be passed, but we should take care not to burn our fingers.

Judge Dee, like his alter ego van Gulik, was no numb-skull, and habitually analysed what was going on. He usually had to deal with criminals and self-willed colleagues and found himself perpetually surrounded by the countless and witless burghers whom he kept order for, but he did meet, once a while, true sages who presented themselves in different shapes. We meet Master Gourd (in *Necklace and Calabash*), a Taoist. The confrontation of Dee and Gourd is most revealing. Dee rides his noble steed through a sinister forest. It's late in the day and the light is about to change. Dee reflects on the 'self,' on who he could really be under his guise of diligent official, and beholds his 'true self' in a figure who rides toward him on the narrow path, a human shape that seems to be, completely, in the most minor details, his very own reflection. Yet there is a basic difference, shrouded somewhere in the evening fog that oozes between trees and bushes. Startled and frightened, Dee sees the apparition as the personification of a secret message.

The hallucination withdraws and dull reality takes over. Once both men face each other the difference between them is obvious enough. Judge Dee, the younger and taller man, carries a superior sword, Master Gourd a simple stick. Dee's beautiful horse dominates the sage's little donkey. Dee's leather saddlebags are the sage's gourds, holding mere spring water instead of expensive possessions. But Dee did indeed think that he had seen his own pure essence.

The event weaves through the entire novel, because we are shown that there is, indeed, a reflection. Gourd represents the real value of Dee's individuality but in such a way that the sameness avoids definition. Master Gourd had been a high-ranking official himself but suffered an identity crisis, resigned and became a hermit. Dee knows that he would like to imitate his opponent but sadly admits that his lack of knowledge does not permit such an about-face as yet.

The various scenes depicting both characters are so strongly drawn that we feel that van Gulik is revealing his own struggle.

The much respected ambassador (Japan and The Netherlands are intimately connected in trade and van Gulik's position had to be dizzily high) left a drawer filled with sketches that were all variations on the same theme. In each drawing we see the author alone and crosslegged in a mountain cabin, contemplating emptiness, well away from the self-seeking world. He had mentioned this dream on many occasions and had even looked for a proper site on the slope of Mount Hiey, overlooking vast Lake Biwa near Kyoto, a location favored by many a weary genius, the abode of hermits throughout the ages. He wanted to spend his last years on a blessed spot, busying himself with unbusying his mind, possibly in order to reach the zero condition that once, inexplicably, made the Big Bang, apparently causing a rampant confusion. Master Gourd does confirm this possibility, when Dee asks him how all our troubles came about. *"Emptiness, nothing but emptiness,"* intones the sage, borrowing his text from Taoism's little bible, the *Tao-Te-Ching*, as referred to by van Gulik in his postscript.§

Master Gourd, the Taoist adept, does not officially take disciples, but fate nevertheless places Dee in the position of Gourd's pupil. The plot culminates in a fight where Master Gourd and Dee together take on the dark side that tries to destroy them. Dee is a trained swordsman; he demonstrates a number of intricate moves and eventually manages to strike down some assailants. Meanwhile Gourd, who seems to do nothing, is an even more spectacular victor. The old man is a cripple—his legs were crushed when his horse was killed under him—and

§translation by van Gulik's colleague and friend, Professor J. J. L. Duyvendak (*Wisdom of the East Series*, London, 1954, p. 40).

has been sitting on a stool all that time, gesticulating with his walking stick. He explains to Dee that he had 'emptied' himself so that he could mirror his enemies' every move. Whenever their swords swished, their points were blocked by his cane. In the end, thoroughly exhausted, they all fell on the floor, where he bound and gagged them without any trouble. Still, John Blofeld claims that van Gulik had no idea of the true meaning of a *dorjeh*.

There are other sages in other Dee novels who invariably irritate the judge by making ostensibly innocent remarks that somehow inexplicably connect with his subconscious.

Dee, a strict Confucianist, was the respected representative of moralistic authority. The system he believed in would keep China together for thousands of years. Relativation is never his strong point and only slowly seeps through his reserved defenses. Van Gulik keeps encouraging Dee's individuation by pitting him against spiritual superstars.

The novel *The Chinese Maze Murders* sets Dee against Master Crane Robe and van Gulik doesn't even bother to define this ogre-like cenobite as a Taoist or a Buddhist. Crane Robe lives a luxuriously aesthetic life in a mountain cabin overgrown by splendid orchids, and immediately makes sure that Dee knows that he, the sage, does not admire those who tread the common road. There's an enigmatic dialogue, or rather a monologue (for Dee merely looks stupid), that contains an enlightening poem:

Only two ways lead to the Eternal gate:
Either dig your head in the mud like a worm,

or float high above the this and that
like a swan, in an azure sky.

Dee doesn't know how to be clever with this arrogant guru, and wanders home, mumbling irritably to himself.

Chinese Zen training thought of a game that masters could play with their silly disciples. The master comes up with some apparently incomprehensible riddle, dramatically recites his quote (he usually hasn't thought of it himself), and hits his ignorant disciple while he shouts, "What does it mean, oaf? What does it mean, fathead?" The disciple then faces some humiliating weeks while he is being ridiculed because of his slowness, until he finds another quote (again originality is not appreciated) that can cap the wisdom flung at him by his master.

I spent some time thumbing through books of Eastern Wisdom trying to find a suitable retort to Master Crane Robe's dual choice, until I understood that I could also search in Western Script for the answer. Mr. Natural, as shown by his first disciple, R. Crumb, when asked by his other disciple, Flakey Foont, about the purpose of things, is told by his guru: "Don't mean sheeit . . ."

Dee, however, not yet versed in mystic lore as inspired by the Zen planet Uranus, didn't know enough to cut through duality with the Bodhisatva Manjusri's sword of total oneness.

Dee, tricked by Crane Robe, still believes in one or the other, and sadly reflects that he will have to dig about like a worm, leaving elevated characters like Crane Robe the choice of a gloriously empty sky. Van Gulik must have been depressed by his own repetitious routine that day. The coworker I quoted earlier said that van Gulik would occasionally sigh and regretfully state that he hadn't really escaped from the Dance of the Sabretiger, that seemed to be his karmic destination.

As a final plea toward acceptance of van Gulik's subtle insights I refer to Zen bum Loo, featured as a guest star in *Poets and Murder*. Loo, who poses as a 'sacristan' but never explains which shrineroom of what temple might be his charge, is a master in calligraphy and much appreciated for his clever sayings that he smears on sheets with a broom. The man behaves in an almost studiedly rough manner, is ugly to behold, addresses anyone as an inferior and doesn't care, for he has little to lose. Loo likes to come out with sudden poetry, too, while scratching his stubbly face, farting and belching. He tells the judge:

"We all return from where we came—
To where the flame went when we snuffed the candle."

Judge Dee, unprodded by van Gulik, can't think of a comment and asks formally: "Would you mind telling me what you mean by that?"

"No," says rude Loo.

Here again is a reference to a master/disciple Zen confrontation, with the teacher quoting from a book hidden under his seat. The usual dialogue is:

Master points at burning candle, picks it up, blows it out.

The room is now suddenly dark.

Master's voice (dramatic, in pitch blackness): "Where did the light go?"

Disciple: "Huh?"

The disciple will be eventually required to come up with the proper answer, which is: he brings a match, takes the candle, and lights it. His deed implies that he doesn't care about the philosophical aspect of the snuffed flame at all, but realizes that he has the power of bringing light to darkness himself, so that's what he does. Loo goes one step further, implying that we all return to the source, to the void. This is pretty high wisdom but it doesn't directly refer to Judge Dee's presence; the judge is questioning Loo, hoping to find clues. Dee is all wrought up and Loo grins, shifts his obese body, and stares at the magistrate with his 'bulging unblinking eyes.'

"Don't expect any help from me, Judge. I consider human justice a paltry makeshift, and I shan't lift a finger to catch a murderer! Murderers catch themselves. Run around in circles even narrower than those of others. Never escape!"

Judge Dee (as the bourgeois segment in van Gulik's own character, and that in his readers') becomes irritated by the monk's uncouth ways. Understandably, for a magistrate can't work with foggy theories. Dee subscribes to clear rules, issued by religion and state, and follows well-defined Confucian morals. Life is good. The emperor is our holy father. Order will be. Justice will reign supreme. Duty and diligence and a proper sense of commitment; show respect toward parents, teachers and employers and all will come right. Dee's regulating hand is loving but strong. And here we have this smelly fat fellow with the eye condition, this Zen bum Loo, telling us that we can forget about human justice? The holy men in van Gulik's books make short shrift with the vicious circle of our happy routine, but they're jolly fellows, like van Gulik

himself. He had a good time while he conscientiously
practised scholarly science. He never committed himself
to any particular faith, but certainly didn't ignore, and
surely made good use of the 'numinous' religious aspects
that Blofeld mentioned.

Writers tend to bare some of their usually hidden thoughtlife while the typewriter hums and clacks, so even the respected scholar/diplomat van Gulik may perhaps reveal himself somewhat in his work. In *The Chinese Maze Murders* (1950) sex raises its long inquisitive snout, but in *The Chinese Bell Murders* (1949–1950) the author has definitely slipped into something a little more comfortable for the day. Van Gulik excuses himself, in a note filed away at Boston University, in a Mugar blue box.

"I had to answer [van Gulik writes] *rather a lot of female fanmail, and the ladies kept asking whether Dee couldn't be 'more warmly' sketched. After all, he was a fairly attractive fellow: wide-shouldered, a full flowing beard, etc.—and although he kept three wives at home, he did move about rather a lot outside, so . . . well, I would say that I did my best."*

Checking back through the Judge Dee saga's thousands of pages one may come up with some tempting scenes. Judge Dee wanders about in a pleasure quarter, gathering information re a hideous murder that he has to

solve. A prostitute lets him know that she is volunteering
information that may endanger her own safety. In order
not to compromise the attractive young lady Dee decides
to visit her as a customer would. She strips, and arranges
herself invitingly on her couch. The magistrate just lies
there, composed, both in body and mind. Then there is
another book, another girl, same Dee. He's after implicat-
ing clues again and the young lady takes him out boat-
ing. It's a warm day. The girl chatters away, passes
incriminating information, Dee is all done—it's still a
warm night. The girl wants to cool off, and strips for a
swim. She suddenly remembers something she should
have told the magistrate. Dee is ashore, his boots happen
to be muddy and it takes all his attention and energy to
rub them clean. Dee masters his lower lusts, and van
Gulik, who *is* Dee (he told us), copies this detached activity. The higher self stays pure.

A Chinese magistrate, so we read in one of the many
clarifying prefaces that van Gulik tacked on to his tales,
was a continuously overworked official. His personality
embodied the ultimate authority of the territory assigned
to him by the crown, but he delegated a good deal of his
power to lower ranks. The local cops, whose self-interest
connected them intimately to the population, were not
too reliable, so a magistrate hired his own lieutenants who
followed his service when he was transferred elsewhere.

The lieutenants were a magistrate's arms and legs,
part of his brain, part of his very soul. Dee, an excep-
tional man, wouldn't content himself with ordinary assistants. He earned the very best, and when Ma Joong and
Chiao Tai came his way he recognized them as splendid
fellows. Chiao, a former officer, deserted the army to dis-
associate himself from corrupt superiors. He and Ma

Joong became 'brothers of the green woods,' highwaymen who robbed the rich and helped the poor, and mistook Dee for another lax and lazy official who could be shaken-down for his cash extorted from a suffering population. Both men were good fighters but not as great as Dee. They acknowledged his superior swordsmanship, deduced that only a good man could fight that well, surrendered and applied for jobs.

Van Gulik thoroughly enjoyed describing his lieutenants' adventures. Fantasy is connected to our conscious and subconscious desires. The lieutenants were the more material parts of his favorite hero.

Dee has to constrain his desires for the author couldn't expect his readers to believe that an incorruptible high official of Dee's spiritual stature would slip and slither, but the lieutenants have plenty of leeway and make use of their space, page after page. Within proper limits of course, proper Chinese limits of the times. The lieutenants are top cops but do not abuse their might. Ma Joong likes to embrace servant girls, ladies of pleasure, an artiste here and there, and the erotic togetherness is described in some detail, again, within appropriate limitation. Ma Joong is a jolly fellow; Chiao's yin harmonizing with his yang follows more subtle patterns than Ma's.

Ma is extroverted, Chiao very introverted. Ma heads for a double happy end; toward the end of the series twins await him: two nice girls, well shaped, good cooks, pliable lovers, but no intellectuals. They create a nice home.

Ma has always been a little comical; Chiao tragic. Chiao's end is tragic, too—he dies while he defends Dee against most murky evil. Ma has lusty and funny adventures, Chiao's lovelife is perhaps somewhat perverted. He is a handsome tough male and the ladies go crazy over his muscled tanned body, large quiet eyes, athletic gait, thoughtfulness and good manners. But does he really want to be loved? Chiao must have been born from van Gulik's quiet moods, that he indulged when he walked silently through picturesque alleys of inner cities, or while he withdrew to his study, or sat in a hidden corner of the embassy's garden, holding hands with an equally withdrawn gibbon. Together they listened to the wind in the pine trees.

There's a poem about that cool evening wind on a hot summer day. *Hama no matsukaze,* translated by van Gulik:

'Will she come? Will she come?' I thought
Wandering along the beach—
But there was nothing but the whispering wind
In the pinetrees.

Who are we human males ultimately longing for? The final beloved, who'll pass the divine answer, and while she embraces us, the veil of ignorance will part so that we can become angels together. Chiao must have looked for *her* and he probably found her while he died, experienced the final liberation while he handled Dee's famous sword during his last fight.

A detective friend and a fan of Judge Dee told me that he suspected van Gulik of having had a very hectic and disturbing affair with twin sisters, or, in any case, look-alike sisters. Ma gets his twins but Chiao, and that was what made my policeman friend look up, but Chiao, van Gulik's other intimate projection, *also* gets involved with twins.

Murder in Canton shows us how Chiao meets the

lovely, witty, superbly artistic and abstract twin sisters
Dananir and Dunyazad, half-Chinese half-Persian. They
are linguists (amazing) and know their way inside/out
two Chinese dialects, Persian and Arabic. They do everything within their subtle powers to seduce Chiao, and do
make some headway, but Chiao, the dreamer in a separate reality, finds their doubled charms just a little too
pushy, and gracefully withdraws.

"Listen," my friend from Homicide said. "I can buy one
pair of fantasy twins, even *I* ran into duplicated pleasure
once, but it didn't become a big thing, I didn't marry
them for God's sake. Ma did, right? And Ma is the rough
side, okay? But Chiao, Chiao interests me, Chiao is the
quiet fellow, and the better one, if you ask me. He's the
guy who defends his boss, his owner, *himself*— follow?—
saves the judge's life and all, loses his own in the process.
And Chiao almost goes for twins, too? Nah. There must be
some real twins somewhere."

Maybe. Maybe there were. They'd be old ladies by now.
Van Gulik would be 76 today. It's all a long time ago, a
tender memory, hidden under other memories, that they
joined, and became fertile soil together, like the forest
floor consisting of a million leaves. I said that to my detective friend. "Yeh," he said thoughtfully, "twins, man.
But subject couldn't have married them both. It isn't in
our law. But in China?"

So far the pleasurable side of love—van Gulik also
treats the unpleasant side. Many of the bad guys beaten
down by Dee are sexually deformed, and some of the
crimes he investigates are caused by twisted sexual de-
sire. Crime literature often makes use of this swamp of
perversion, but in van Gulik's novels we can believe what
he tells us. Each case he uses did really happen in China

one time, and has been exhaustively researched and correctly analysed. He mentions the main plot of *The Haunted Monastery* in a magazine article (*Boekenkorf,* June 1961):

"It stands to reason that much of what I experienced during my many years in the Orient can be used in my novels. The illustration [we see an older Chinese man in a wide robe, and a silken hat, who has a long narrow face and pensive eyes that peer calmly into the camera] *shows a powerful monk whom I met in Peking, 1946, after I was transferred out of Chungking where I stayed during the war. I was in the great and famous Taoist monastery called "The White Clouds," in Po-yün. The snapshot was taken in one of the hundreds of pavilions that make up that immense temple. You see the abbot An Shih-lin. I always rather liked the man but I heard later that he had a habit of abusing young girls that were unfortunate enough to wander within his reach, and he was burned alive later on by orthodox monks. By that time the communist army was marching toward Peking and the general confusion prevented a proper investigation. I did reflect on the matter, however, and the facts underly my novel."*

I found the book disturbing, especially when I realized that the various mental and physical tortures did truly happen and that van Gulik was fully qualified to describe the shadowside of the Chinese mind. It would even have been easier for van Gulik than for a proper Chinese to describe these foul and fascinating scenes, for as a foreigner he could observe without feeling too personally involved, so that his vision would be clearer.

The University of Chicago published the four main novels of the Judge Dee series (*The Chinese Lake, Bell, Nail and Gold Murders*) as part of its China program. *Sexual Life in Ancient China* is also kept in print (Brill, Leyden). Literature and the various branches of psychology are complementary disciplines and van Gulik probably spent more time and effort on studying the Chinese sexual drive than any other western sinologue. He privately published a 242 page essay entitled *Erotic Colour Prints of the Ming Period, with an Essay on Chinese Sex Life from the Han to the Ch'ing Dynasty, B.C. 206 to A.D. 1644,* reserving the edition to fifty copies that he presented to colleagues all over the world. I found one at Columbia University, and spent a number of pleasant hours reading the meticulous text in van Gulik's precise and clear handwriting. The portfolio (1951) is of special value, as relatively little is known about Chinese erotic prints, while much attention has been paid to the Japanese style of erotic art that was inspired by them. Until the beginning of this century Japanese brides were given picture books of the *'variegated positions of the flowery battle'* so that they might share a better time with their marital partners. Once they went out of proper use these books were considered to be pornographic literature and collected as such by connoisseurs. Van Gulik points out that the idea is quite erroneous. The Chinese prints that came his way as a lucky find (or rather the printing blocks from which he manufactured his own pictures) are of extreme interest for various other quite innocuous reasons, he assures us. Firstly, they are among the finest examples of Chinese colorprinting, an artform with a brief history, for it rose and fell between 1570 and 1640, developing from diffident first attempts via perfection to final decadence, and traveling from the more austere north of Peking to the indulgent, and also mentally much warmer, 'lesser capital,' Nanking. Then, as the author points out, only in

**The Old Immortal about to Penetrate the Jade Gate
(from the instructive portfolio *Hua-ying-chin-chen*
[Variegated Positions of the Flowery Battle])**

these erotic drawings can we see that the Chinese artists did, in fact, know (it has often been assumed that Chinese art skipped the nude altogether) how to draw completely undressed human figures. Also, the author claims, there is a useful sociological aspect. By studying the pictures we become aware of intimate clothing "such as undergarments, socks, leggings, etc.," that are not normally shown in Chinese paintings. Moreover, there is furniture in the drawings, providing information on the interior decoration of that past period. There is also medical interest in the various love and lust positions, van Gulik tells us.

As his devoted fan I want to believe him.

The texts that accompany this type of ancient art are, to today's eyes, maybe amusing. We see and hear about the experienced head of the family, with his wives, female servants, slavegirls, welcoming a new item to his collection. The title of the picture and poem is 'Shooting a Chicken,' and describes the first sexual encounter of the official rogue and a virgin girl. Ha! Excuse me. This isn't pornographic, this is educative to young future wives. All right. They will, the poem has it, "find it hard to contain themselves while clear secretions spring up in their Jade Well,' and the husband is introduced to us as like the 'Old Immortals' (who were, and are, being immortal, always ready to jump, as we read in old Chinese legends), whose 'passion knows no mercy, whose erected member strains his belt.' There is a sinister ending. 'Blood,' the poem sighs compassionately, 'will flow.'

Okay, okay, all very educative, but what to think of Buddhist monks visiting their parishioners in their private quarters and, well, really . . . (see illustration, the young man with the shaven head is the monk). Buddhist

The Buddhist Monk Instructing a Parishioner (from the instructive portfolio *Hua-ying-chin-chen [Variegated Positions of the Flowery Battle]*)

monks always had a peculiar reputation in ancient China, with their preference for fornication rather than meditation, and their sly ways of not paying taxes on vast wealth, swindled out of a superstitious populace. The monk, we hear in the accompanying poem, is like 'the straying bee intent on sucking,' and he's in luck for 'the heart of the peony is about to open.'

The treatise contains unillustrated poetry too that represents the attitude of young beauties ready and willing to enter their future husband's quarters, chanting about 'their good opportunity' (to meet with this high-class and wealthy fellow), 'how they hanker after the first union,' 'long to be like the bedmat,' and act as 'cover to protect him from draughts and cold.' How she will sit on the bed and diligently study 'the picture scroll by the side of the pillow' and take off her robes before 'practising all the exciting postures,' but one wonders whether her mother really gave her the picture of the monk/bee working on the devout lady/peony. After all, infidelity on the woman's part (a man couldn't commit adultery for he was free to do as he pleased) was a serious crime.

China, a prudish country today, although loosening up again, had on occasion been free and happy in its sexual usages, until, after the T'ang dynasty (Judge Dee's period) narrow-mindedness came in. Van Gulik blames re-examiners of ancient Confucian classics, who misinterpreted outmoded taboos relative to keeping the sexes apart. So the shadow of something like Calvinism fell in the tenth century. More advanced ideas took over again, especially during the fifteenth and sixteenth centuries, and were squashed once more, under the rule of the Manchus—not, surprisingly, because of the will of the Manchu Emperors, but due, rather, to strongly restrictive attitudes of the Chinese themselves, that they managed to impose on the foreign rulers.

Van Gulik pleads throughout his manuscript that the prudish Chinese behavior during the nineteenth, and even the twentieth, centuries, did not, as some Western observers claimed, cover up *'a cesspool of dire depravity.'* The author, on the contrary, admires a happy activity that went on in private, although he admits to some perversions, noticeably in corrupt Taoist circles, where depraved magic made use of female slaves to extract the *'elixir of long life,'* while practising a cruel sexual vampirism. There was, in Chinese society, no trace of, for instance, flagellation, which became popular in the West, and S & M games were never appreciated. This is amazing, we hear, when we realize that Chinese upper class men usually controlled wives and mistresses, and attractive lower class servants that they owned outright. The conclusion, van Gulik draws from a number of arguments, is, emphatically, that the ancient Chinese never had any reason to be ashamed of their sex life.

And they weren't, of course. There is a certain delicate feeling, like of never showing female naked (bound) feet, for the distortions that Chinese ladies of class had to suffer in order to develop a certain attractive way of walking, made their naked feet look rather gruesome. Delicacy, no shame.

And neither should van Gulik himself be ashamed of his fervent interest in these matters. To the pure all is pure, and he quotes the *Bhagavat Gita* (on the very first page of the portfolio)

The Lord said:
He who can behold Me in all things and

all things in Me, he shall never lose
Me nor shall I ever lose him.

The label of 'literary pornographer' that was stuck to van
Gulik's back during the fifties—still a prudish time in
Western Europe—irritated him tremendously. I happened to run into a Swedish professor, teaching Chinese
at Columbia University, who met Dr. van Gulik just once.
The two scholars arranged that they would spend a few
days in each others' company to study some obscure writings, but both airplanes were delayed and they only had
a few minutes together. Van Gulik found time to make
one significant remark. "Professor," he said solemnly, "I
am an ardent admirer of pure eroticism."

He was interested in other activities, too, for sex is not
the only motivation of our busyness down below. Whoever studies another civilization will soon be struck by
the appearance of enforceable laws. Van Gulik's studies
in this respect culminated in his translation and discussion of a thirteenth century handbook for magistrates,
the *T'ang-Yin-Pi-Shih*, that he translated as *Parallel Cases
from under the Pear-tree.*

7

Dr. van Gulik's chest trouble was, again, in 1967, diagnosed as a complex symptom of a serious disease, and he finally paid heed and had himself flown to The Hague for a second opinion and, possibly, curative treatment. By then he must have felt the end approach for he took the trouble to dictate extensive notes that were stenciled into a 30 page pamphlet. He explains the origins of the Dee books but also formulates some creative thoughts:

"I am glad," van Gulik writes, *"that my British publisher Heinemann asked me to keep going with the series, for it has become clear to me that this activity has become an important part of my work during the last fifteen years. It has, in a way, become of equal importance as the time I have spent on scientific research. Practising sinology made it possible for me to continue my diplomatic career, for in diplomacy we are always busy with most temporary matters; scientific research offers a pleasant alternative, an escape even, for in science everything we do is of some permanent value, even the mistakes which we make, for they will enable others to do a better job later. However, in*

*science, especially if we make a serious effort, we become
slaves of facts and any imagination must be strictly
avoided. While writing his novels an author is free to create his own facts and can fantasize as much as he pleases.
That is why writing my 'thrillers' has become a most necessary third aspect of my work, a relaxation that keeps my
interest in diplomatic and scientific activities alive."*

So what is he saying here? That, in order to fulfill a
family-inflicted purpose, he has to be a diplomat? And that
he is bored with diplomatic cocktail parties? That, in order
to escape from professional trivialities he likes to with-
draw into scholastic research? That bored with scratching
dry facts into brittle paper he escapes again into novel
writing? Only in his novels he becomes free, in the guise of
Judge Dee? Free from what? Free from ego dragging?

Not quite true, perhaps. Any honest novelist will reluc-
tantly admit that he is the slave of his own creation, the
characters that he himself has rubbed into life. Van Gulik was still restricted by Judge Dee's strict morals and
conceit that served as an armored corset, self-inflicted to
defend a self. So van Gulik escaped again. Very likely
even a good straight Dee became a demon, who pushed
his author into moving on. So van Gulik now projects
himself as a solitary ruminator, a Buddhist using Confucianist discipline to pursue the Tao and realize his inner
freedom. Here we have the drawings of the lone spirit
watching unruffled Lake Biwa from his hermitage on the
slopes of Mount Hiey.

"Nothing but emptiness," says Master Gourd.

"Floating like a swan in an azure sky," says Master
Crane.

"Return to the origin, where the light goes, from the
candle you have snuffed," advises Zen-bum Loo.

The advice seems to point at the ultimate religious experience where we give up our soul, and everything we are with it, but van Gulik was still writing. Masters Gourd and Crane Robe were still busy too, doing their holyman-routine, because the relative, Samsara, is merely the other side of the absolute, Nirvana. They act wise, the Free Spirits, secretly admired by Dee, but they stay stuck, while alive. Gourd travels about endlessly, on his tired little donkey. Crane Robe grows a new crop of orchids to decorate his rural palace, and Loo has to fill up white sheets with the black smudges of his ego-broom. Wise men, nevertheless, all of them, who taught van Gulik, and eventually us. Wise men of the highest level, sages, adepts, enlightened creatures who wear their humanity as a mask. Hard to follow, these superior beings.

Van Gulik's work also includes a book on wise men of a lower category, a level of life where logic still applies. He introduces a new set of teachers in *Parallel Cases from under the Pear-tree*, a manual of jurisprudence and detection. This anthology of famous antique Chinese law cases was edited by attorney Kuei Wan-jung, in 1211. Kuei's exemplary men are all ancient magistrates who, according to the preface, want nothing more than to *'revenge evil, see the truth by ripping away lies, entice demons from their dark dungeons, bring criminals to justice, ascertain life and death by feeling the pulse, and polish the mirror of impartiality so that it will properly reflect both beauty and ugliness.'*

Most readers will not quarrel with these idealizations, but they may look up when Kuei talks about 'the ideal state.' We are back with pure spirituality again for, in Taoist terms, the ideal ruler does not rule. *'Seated on his throne facing South, sunk in mediation, he is the link*

棠 陰 比 事

T'ANG-YIN-PI-SHIH

"PARALLEL CASES FROM UNDER THE PEAR-TREE"

A 13TH CENTURY MANUAL OF
JURISPRUDENCE AND DETECTION

TRANSLATED FROM THE ORIGINAL CHINESE
WITH AN INTRODUCTION AND NOTES

BY

R. H. VAN GULIK, LITT. D.

(高 羅 佩)

LEIDEN
E. J. BRILL
1956

between Heaven and Earth, ensuring peace and order solely by the aura of his virtue.'

So, no trouble? But there was—van Gulik helps Kuei explain—then like now, a shortage of sages, and kings were fools. Their laws and the instruments of their enforcement were 'things reeking of vulgarity' that should be ignored by scholar-officials of refined taste.

That they were not wise proves that these vulgar laws were necessary, even if they were but faulty reflections of the True Code 'that never should be uttered, as she lives quietly, deep in the true insight of every man.'

Enough of the 'shoulds' 'mights' and 'woulds,' for we deal here with reality on our own low level, and *Parallel Cases* is a brilliant collection of 144 criminal cases, so cleverly solved that they can even guide us today.

Van Gulik also used some of them himself. Any avid reader of the Dee saga recalls the judge finding a corpse without being able to ascertain the cause of death. Dee, himself not without knowledge of medicine, calls in the coroner, an experienced 'pathologist,' but cannot find out what killed his man.

To complicate matters Judge Dee (already married to three ladies) falls in love, with the coroner's lovely and intelligent wife. She loves him, too. She also loves her husband who is both a good man and a hunchback. A very tricky business this, for the detective cannot love his suspect. Now what if she were to become a suspect?

The coroner's wife saves Dee, who gets himself in deep trouble by having a suspect, another intelligent lady, tortured. Torture of suspects is all right according to ancient Chinese law, provided the suspect has really committed the crime. Physical (and mental) abuse can be helpful in extracting a full confession. Without a confession there can be

迹賊

唐中書舍人郭正一破平壤得二高麗婢名
玉素極姝好也音律艷令專知財物廩正一夜須
漿水粥非二玉素莫之不可二玉素乃壽之良久

於此一節亦有取焉耳
也文案整密不可得反難二酷吏無足道然
際戒在疏略是故慎史稱嚴延年之治獄
其情則後必讎異而毒人得計矢推讞之
鄭克曰凡善讞獄者必善覘情也若不得
亦欲為二他日讎異跳死之計爾土官沂絲
儔年不得瞥而為坐客二既爭且其後必數尚

Hayashi Dōshun's copy of the *Parallel Cases*, one
page comprising the end of Case 8-A and the
beginning of Case 8-B

no verdict. Dee knows intuitively that a man has been
murdered and that the murderer is his wife, but she
won't give in. She now charges her magistrate with im-
proper behavior and Dee, accused of unnecessary and
therefore willful torture, may lose his own head. There is
a stalemate—Dee's superiors frown, the population mur-
murs. Then the coroner's wife whispers. She tells him to
check the corpse's skull. There were no X-rays in those
days, and Dee couldn't know that a long thin needle had
been hammered into the unfortunate man's head. How
did the coroner's wife know?

Dee finds that he has solved two murders. The coroner's wife, a former widow, killed her first husband in the
same horrible way.

What can Dee do? Charge the beautiful refined lady
(her first husband was a drunken lout) whom he, moreover, loves (and cannot marry, for he respects her present
husband) with a crime that can only be atoned by death?
He frets.

She kills herself.

A most subtle and truly horrible plot, refining the 'human predicament' (are we really forced to commit evil?)
that van Gulik lifted from *Parallel Cases* and deftly used
himself. Many of his other tales revolve around examples
borrowed from the obscure material. He always tells us,
of course, in footnotes, prefaces or postscripts, about the
origins of his inspiration. The book is out of print but I
ran into a copy and used some of the plots myself.†
(There are still some left).

---

†*Inspector Saito's Small Satori* (Putnam, 1985; Ballantine, 1987)

In order to give an idea of how the plots are phrased I've selected some at random:

Case 6 B

"When the Minister Li Nan-kung was Judicial Intendent in Hopei, a minor official had committed a crime and was put in prison. When interrogated he did not confess, keeping his mouth closed he did not eat for more than a hundred days. The prison officials did not dare to question him under torture lest they came to harm in the extreme case [of the weakened prisoner dying on their hands]. Li Nan-kung said: 'I can make him eat immediately.' He had the prisoner brought before him for questioning and said: 'I shall stop up your nose with something; then will you be able to continue refusing to eat?' The man was greatly afraid, he started eating again (and finally confessed his crime). Now that man was expert in 'feeding on air' [A Taoist discipline]; but if his nose were stopped up, his breathing would be obstructed and the air would cease to circulate. Therefore he confessed."

Case 51 A

"In the [Northern] Chou Dynasty [557–581 A.D.] when Yü Chung-wen was Prefect of Chao, there were two men of the surname Tu and Jen, each of whom lost a cow. Later a (stray) cow was found, and both contended it was theirs. The local authorities could not solve this case. Then the administrator of I-chou called Han Po-hsi said:

'Yü of An-ku proved clever in detecting in his youth. He must be ordered to decide this case.' Yü Cheng-wen had both parties drive their cows to the tribunal. He let loose the stray cow, and it joined Jen's herd. Then he had one of his men inflict a small wound on the cow. Jen sighed with grief while Tu did not show any emotion. Thereupon Tu confessed."

Case 8 A

When the Minister Fan Ch'ung-jen was Prefect of Ho-chung, [his subordinate] the Executive Inspector Sung Tan-nien became ill after a banquet held in his house, and during the night he suddenly died. This was because one of his concubines had illicit relations with a minor officer [and therefore the pair was arrested for further investigation of their possible connection with the sudden death of Sung]. Fan Ch'ung-jen, knowing that it had not been a natural death, ordered the local officials to investigate. During the autopsy it was found that blood had flown from the nine openings of the body. The concubine and the officer said: 'We put poison in the turtle mince-meat.' Fan Ch'ung-jen asked during which course the mincemeat had been served; [when he learned that this had occurred early in the banquet] he said: 'How could the poisoned man have sat through the entire banquet? This is certainly not the truth!' He ordered a further investigation. Then it transpired that when the guests were leaving, the accused had murdered Sung by placing poison in his wine cup. Since Sung did not eat turtle mince-meat and since the other guests had rejected it also, the criminals had hoped that later the case would have to be reopened on different premises and that they thusly would escape the death penalty."

Human nastiness cannot have changed all that much— it's quite easy to enter the world of a Chinese judge during the seventh century. Methods did change. Warfare between Good and Evil couldn't use computers, chemical laboratories, instantaneous information bounced off a satellite during the T'ang dynasty. There were psychological tricks, however. Judge Dee, aware of subconscious fears in his suspects, sometimes dresses up as a magistrate from the Netherworld, and sneaks into their jail cells, followed by his lieutenants who wear masks of animal demons. He also exhausts his victims and then suddenly, and casually, approaches them as a 'well-meaning friend.' Fortunately he's basically good, so we can always accept his *modus operandi.*

Spooky stuff—there were real spooks too. Classic Chinese tales often have ghosts bear witness, even in court, but van Gulik limits himself to showing them (mostly) in illusions. When ghosts appear to Judge Dee the procedure is as follows:

1. The ghost draws Dee's attention. Dee is suitably frightened. The ghost's activity seems to indicate illegal business here or there.

2. The judge checks the indicated situation and locates a suspect. There's, for the time being, no more mention of the ghost. The plot unravels; suspect is found guilty. Any proof is legal and above board. Causes and effects connect logically throughout. At the end of the tale the ghost

is mentioned again but Dee manages to prove that he (the spook) wasn't really there. In one case there was a paper lantern with a dirty spot. The light in the lampion projected the spot as a likeness of a human being that was silhouetted on a white garden wall. A sudden wind blew through a tube and caused near-human sounds. Nothing really went on. The reader can go to bed and sleep soundly tonight.

3. Then, when all is just about good, *the ghost suddenly reappears*, and thanks the judge.

Dee was an historical figure, and the Dee books center in historical plots. So van Gulik was not original? He certainly was, for nobody could ever match his brilliant, and original, combinations, all based on minute scholarly work.

Van Gulik did, however, later in his too-short life, come up with a novel in which a modern fictitious Dutchman solves a contemporary crime. *The Given Day*‡ is mostly set in Amsterdam, shortly after WW II. There is a connection with the Orient, for the novel's hero has been maltreated by the Japanese in Java, and there is also a link with the Middle East, where van Gulik was stationed for several years.

---

‡First published in the U.S. in a 300 copy hardcover edition (Dennis McMillan Publications, 1984). First U.S. paperback edition published December, 1986 (Dennis McMillan Publications).

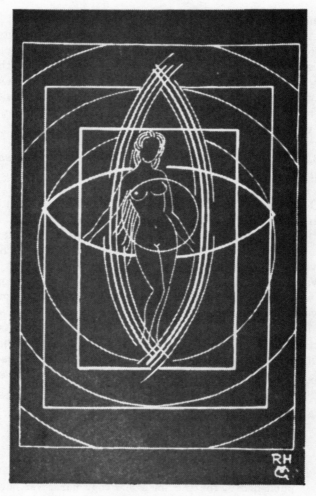

Illustration drawn by van Gulik for
The Given Day (page 30)

8

"I *am* Dee," van Gulik told a colleague novelist, while discussing the art of literature in an Amsterdam bar. No doubt he was close to being right; all his statements were habitually based on scientific research, and subconscious experiences are mentioned in many of his notes.

Each man—the Greeks knew it for the Egyptians had told them—is *legio*. Our personalities are complex.

Van Gulik also acknowledged, and confirmed, his 'Dutch gentleman' (split-)personality. It dominated his stage, with his permission, whenever he resided in The Netherlands. The Dutch Literary Museum, The Hague, has filed some interviews that bear witness to this role.

He is a large man, the newspaper, already yellow with age, tells us, *dressed casually in a grayish-green three piece suit, and he sports a boyish red checked necktie. His roundish face (dark eyes behind miniature glasses held by a gold frame) seems mysterious somehow, and is hard to fit within one of the better known categories of our fellow human beings. The small mustache and goatee enhance that effect.*

Mysterious? How so? The reporter seems to have no trouble in drawing out the important personage.

Van Gulik talks easily, without a trace of self-importance that one might expect, considering his high and exotic status. We hear that he doesn't remember his early youth in the provincial town of Zutphen, except for one event— he fell into a pond. He also mentions an eye operation. He was blind for several weeks but enjoyed himself, watching 'well-focused pictures my mind kept projecting.' The memories, showing up as well-plotted movies, fascinated him and he almost regretted having his sight back again.

The year was 1964. He was busy working at the Ministry of Foreign Affairs, had a good time at home (Ten Hovestraat 88, The Hague, a comfortable residence), his 'hobbies' took up most of his spare moments and, he assured the reporter, he was visiting his clubs. Another interview supplies us with their names. There was the *The Hague Art Circle*; the society that catered to ex-residents of the island of Java, *Tong Tong*; the select gentleman's club *Pulchri*; and finally a get-together by the name of *Daily Discipline Results in Knowledge*.

All very 'Netherlandish,' meaning kind of low, constricted. How did he feel, hooked and tied? Shouldn't he tell us? In a novel?

He did, in *The Given Day*, subtitled 'An Amsterdam Mystery,' Volume #49 in van Hoeve's forgotten series of 'Kramer's Pockets.' The Dutch translation, a friendly bookseller told me, immediately 'misfired' and was remaindered. The original English version was privately published in Malaysia, never distributed, and most copies got lost. "Even so," the bookseller said, "I liked the book." He lent me his own copy.

The first U.S. edition (1984) was only published in 300

copies. A paperback edition published in late 1986 will hopefully reach a wider readership.

Van Gulik invites us to identify with another aspect of his character, in the guise of a Dutch ex-colonial official, repatriated after WW II. Mr. Hendriks, a man in his early forties, rents a dismal room in Amsterdam. The wallpaper peels, the paint on the ceiling flakes. There are persistent smells of his landlady's cooking. The weekend is sliding along and our hero has nothing to do, apart from being scared. His fears make him kneel in his bathroom. He hallucinates. His Japanese prison camp guards are closeby—evil shadows, in the alley outside. More of them move through the drizzle on canal quays. It wasn't that long ago that Army Reserve Captain Hendriks was being starved and beaten. Captain Uyeda, of the Japanese Military Police (the dreaded Kempetai) had been erroneously convinced that our Hendriks was a different Hendriks, a spy, who knew secrets. Uyeda patiently tried to pry them out, unwilling to admit that they might be transparent. Even torture becomes boring in the end and the two captains converse when there's occasion for a break. Uyeda tells his victim about the days that he was a Zen student back home. Tough Zen discipline has never been strong on compassion, and its method of immobile and lengthy meditation—in drafty temples where monkish guards stalk, beating the weak-minded—was incorporated in the training of the Japanese Gestapo. The discipline was complete, the sadistic policemen were even issued with a true Zen master. The master saw the students, one by one, and asked them riddles, the famous Zen koans. A proper answer means instant enlightenment, a liberation from ego-constriction, supplies entry into *nirvana* where, because nothing can be lost, anything is gained.

Mr. Hendricks professed interest. It's better to engage in abstract discussion than be kicked in the groin. So what was the honorable Mr. Military Police Captain's superb, inimitable, most superior riddle?

The Japanese officer is sad. He never answered the riddle, didn't pass the koan, never lost the restrictions of his narrow self. His master told him to *make the snow on Mount Fuji melt.*

"But it's eternal snow!"

"Right."

"You can't make it melt."

"Right." Not logically. Not within the limitations of the human mind. The snow will melt, though. Nothing is constant. Everything is a dream. Life is a dream within a dream. We have to wake from it, become free from rebirth, from the wheel of karma that dips us back into pain, again and again.

Nothing is constant indeed. Van Gulik knew that. He lost his art collection. He was always being transferred. When he wrote about Mr. Hendriks he himself was slowly being killed by tobacco smoke. Captain Uyeda was dying too, with his head in a noose, put there by British liberators who had found the Japanese police officer guilty of unpardonable war crimes.

Mr. Hendriks says goodbye to his ex-tormentor, wishes him a good trip, without malice. Captain Uyeda repays his former victim's compassion and presents him with his own unsolved koan. While the Japanese gurgles in the struggle of death the Dutchman mumbles, committing the holy mountain's snow to memory.

What's this? The unfeeling irreligious novelist van Gulik (as John Blofeld, the Buddhist scholar, claimed) is passing the key from a Buddhist to a Christian, who later in the book becomes involved with a gang of Moslems (a devout evil sheik and his criminal but believing henchmen). There is constant soul-searching for all characters concerned before Hendriks is allowed to become a true hero; and like most heroes in the detective genre, he can then claim a prize at the end of the book, a beautiful lady. She offers her attractions but he sets her free so that she can fulfill herself with her true love. Poor Hendriks, weary, beaten, badly burned, all on his own in the moist darkness of Amsterdam's inner city, finally dares to lose his self to the void, so that the eternal snow, that froze his soul, may melt.

The Dutch literary reviewers were furious. This was heresy. What was this Zen? Some newfangled religion? They had no idea of what the book was about and classified it as less than a threepenny novel; cheap trash written merely to distract. They went to great lengths to explain that van Gulik's art, in spite of its popularity in foreign countries, could not be 'literature.' What a pity, they added, that some of this perhaps interesting material could not be used by a real writer.

Technically they also tore at the book. How could Hendriks drive a jeep and handle a stengun in 1942, when these machines had not as yet been manufactured? Why did the Arab bandits speak so strangely? They were homosexuals too, weren't they? And how come all this out of the way stuff happened in Holland? Nothing ever happens in Holland.

Nothing much happens in the minds of some reviewers. Van Gulik reveals himself more in this book than in any other of his most intimate writings. Hendriks' mask fits van Gulik easier than Judge Dee's. In order to understand the human problem in ancient China the author had to make more of an effort than to merely step out into a Dutch scene set yesterday. Judge Dee cannot slip into a Dutch bar, sniff the *fragrance of Dutch gin, moist clothes, tobacco and sawdust* and *find a spot between an elbow covered in blue corduroy and another in threadbare tweed.* Like Hendriks, van Gulik sipped Dutch gin from high-stemmed tulip shaped glasses in the filtered light of an antique bar. Van Gulik must have wondered there about his rapidly approaching death, while his projection, Hendriks, would still be around, winning psychological battles in the minds of his readers.

Another Dutch writer, who met van Gulik in one of these bars, told me that the ambassador reminded him of an eagle, coming down to the barnyard chickens, to tell them they were all birds. "He talked about Buddhism some," the writer said. "Gloomy stuff, you know, but it seemed to cheer him up."

Perhaps it was the ultimate freedom which is within that made van Gulik smile while he conversed with fellow artists. The Tao must have cheered him somewhat, in spite of his coughing and the pain in his chest.

There was the poem that Judge Dee discovered in *The Lacquer Screen*, that made him thoughtful, although it didn't belong to his government's creed:

Being born means to have to suffer
Living and Suffering are identical ideas
Dying, and never being born again
Is the only way out
The final way out, away from unpleasantness, from pain.

Judge Dee, a moralist, and Hendriks, raised as a Christian, both liked these ideas that show our 'reality' as another illusion. They both were solitary heroes, potential immortal aspects of van Gulik, the 'large man with the mysterious manner'; aspects that went far beyond the short arms of his contemporary critics.

So much for *The Given Day* at a lofty level. It has a lower level too, filled with rough action that keeps us busy. Three of the bad guys die and the forth is arrested. All ends well and we can go back to sleep while the true quest continues.

Van Gulik's thrillers were fairly popular in Holland between 1959 and 1967, but subsequently disappeared. When they were republished in the seventies every volume was a bestseller. Why? An aggressive publisher can, through advertising and proper marketing, achieve some results, but if the public doesn't care even professional salesmanship loses out. What, suddenly, motivated Dutch readers that they wanted to follow an antique Chinese judge? Did they expect to be thrilled into relaxation? Did the exotic effect turn them on? Was there a general interest in things Chinese? Did their minds long for adventures in 'another galaxy a long time ago,' which, in this case, happened to be historically true?

For all these reasons probably, and also because of van Gulik's reputation of being a scholar interested in the bizarre and in sex. The Netherlands enjoyed a violent sexual revolution after centuries of severe Protestant repression. The general public vaguely knew that our ambassador to the Far East had written a tome called *Sexual Life in Ancient China*. Sex tourism had become in vogue and Dutch males were flown to the Orient by the Jumbo, but their pleasures were superficial and there may have been a demand for proper guidance.

There may be a connection here. Western guilt feelings could see their reflection in the T'ang dynasty where sex was taboo but made available in a large number of guises. Chapter 9 of *Sexual Life in Ancient China* records some guidelines which are illustrative of the attitudes of the time. Penalties were listed in 'points;' the higher their numbers the more awful the punishments the judges could inflict.

committed against/ nature of sin	married women	widows and virgins	nuns	prostitutes
pao-yin "violent debauch," i.e. possessing a woman against her will without really caring for her, and only to display one's wealth and power	500 if servants' wives: 200	1000 if servants' widows, or maids: 500	countless demerits	50 applies when she is unwilling because she has a fixed patron, or other attachment
ch'ih-yin "crazed debauch," i.e. motivated by blind passion	200 if servants' wives: 100	500 if servants' widows, or housemaids: 200	1000	100

committed against/ nature of sin	married women	widows and virgins	nuns	prostitutes
yüan-yeh-yin "predestined debauch," i.e. illicit inter- course with mutual consent, of a man and a woman predes- tined to meet	100 if servants' wives: 50	200 if servants' widows, or house- maids: 100	500	20
hsüan-yin "proclaiming debauch," i.e. talking to others about the above sins	50	100	200	5
wang-yin "idle debauch," i.e. averring that one has sinned as above, while in fact one has not	50	200	100	10

Don't be soft on the sinner, but there was more—like Confucious' admonitions re the following *crimes*:

Going to bed early and rising late (so as to devote much time to sexual dalliance) 1
Encouraging one's women to devote much time to their make-up
. . . . 1

To watch frivolous theatrical plays, every time 1
    Taking part in same 50
Talking frivolously to one's women, without lewd intent 1
    If with intent to excite lust 20
If one's women engage in frivolous talk, not to restrain them . . 1
    If one allows himself to become excited thereby 10
Praising the virtue of one's women . . . . none
Praising their talent and ability 1
Praising their skill in embroidery, sewing, etc. 2
Praising their wisdom and generous nature 5
Telling one's women about some love-affair 10
    If done with the intent to incite lustful thoughts in them . . 20
Telling smutty stories in order to excite them 20
    Exception: If one tells such stories in order to develop the
    women's sense of shame . . . . none
Reading love-poetry in front of one's women 5
    If done in order to excite their lust 20
Reading poetry that extols profound passion, every time 10
    If done to educate one's women . . . . none
Talking to one's women about their make-up, hairdress, personal
    adornment, etc. 1
Showing them exaggerated politeness 1

Surely sufficient to erect priests and parsons, but there
were also *crimes punishable by death*, to wit:

Offending against one's parents or ancestors 1000
Violating a chaste woman 1000
Causing the death of a human being 1000
Selling a house-maid as a prostitute 1000
Infanticide 1000
Producing erotic books, songs, or pictures 1000
    (Same demerits for publishing them)
Slandering a virtuous woman 500

And the T'ang dynasty knew *regular crimes too*, punishable by being beaten and/or lengthy sojourns in jail:

Keeping an excessively large number of wives and concubines
. . . . 50
Showing preference for one of one's women 10
    If this includes encouraging the preferred person to be rude
to the others 20
Comparing the charms of one's womenfolk 1
Gloating over the charms of one's womenfolk 1
Exciting lustful thoughts in oneself 10
Showing one's nakedness when easing nature in the night . . . 1
Lewd dreams, every time 1
    If such a dream occasions a lewd action 5
Singing frivolous songs 2
Studying such songs 20
Reading novels and other light literature 5
Using frivolous language 2
    If no women are present 1
    If done with the intent to excite lust in women 10
Touching the hands of one's womenfolk while handing things to
    them 1
    If with lustful intent 10
    Exception: if done to assist them in case of emergency . . none
    But then if such touching excites lust 10
Not yielding the way to a woman in the street 1
    If at the same time one looks at the woman 2
    If one looks longingly after her 5
    If one conceives lewd thoughts about her 10
Carrying on one's person aphrodisiac incense 1
Burning the same 1
Entering one's women's quarters without warning 1
Associating with friends addicted to whoring and gambling . . 50
Joking about women 50
Joking about gods and deities 30

Speaking dirty language 10
Burning another's house 500
Scheming to make a widow or nun one's concubine 500
Showing preference for one special wife or concubine 500
Abortion 300
    If done to conceal an illicit relation 600
Taking another man whoring or gambling 300
Encouraging a man to sell his wife 300
Not restraining a wife when she maltreats a concubine,
depending on the seriousness of each case .... 100 to 300
    If the maltreatment results in the death of the victim .. 1000
Failure to marry off maid-servants 200
Sporting with a prostitute or catamite, every time 50
Having licentious theatrical plays performed, every time ... 20
Drinking to intoxication 1
Not keeping men and women separate in one's household ... 3
Throwing away a piece of inscribed paper 5
Reading a book with dirty hands 3
Keeping books or inscribed fans in one's bed 3

Still other activities were strenuously disallowed, and
the general idea was that "women invited sin." "The less
talent in a woman," the sage said, "the more virtuous she
will be." All this was Confucianism at its worst, perverted
to suit the pseudo-holiness of the ruling classes. Advanced magistrates like Dee ignored power games that
benefit the mighty, but they were smart enough not to
criticize tradition. If magistrates made waves their own
heads would float, but while, for appearance's sake, there
might be some indulgence in moralizing, the good judge
would rely more on being a good example than on crip-
pling his subjects by painful restrictions. The ideal state,
the refined judges maintained, was kept healthy by non-
interference.

Van Gulik quotes from other scriptures, a little less pompous, somewhat more practical. A governmental scholar writes in 1360:

"There are nine classes of professional women who, if allowed to frequent one's women's quarters, will cause untold troubles, and they divide in the three aunts and the six crones.

The three aunts are the Buddhist nun, the Taoist nun, and the female fortune teller. The six crones are the procuress, the female go-between, the sorceress, the female thief, the female quack, and the midwife. These are indeed like the three punishments and the six harmful cosmic influences. Few are the households which, having admitted one of them, will not be ravaged by fornication and robbery. The men who can guard against those, keeping them away as if they were snakes and scorpions, those men shall come near the method for keeping their households clean."

The onus is still on the female aspect and the man who composed this tirade was a gent from the capital, no doubt an eager client of the twenty thousand prostitutes who earned their bowl of rice in that hub of the universe. Blaming women—so what did the ladies think? Van Gulik quotes a court lady, Kuan, a noble woman known for her poetry:

Poem about You and Me

Between you and me
There's too much emotion
Causing our red hot shouting matches.

Choose activity instead:
Take some clay and shape it so that it resembles you
Take some more clay and make it look like me
Smash both statues and mix the rubble
Again make your own likeness, again make mine
My clay contains yours
Yours contains mine—
Alive we sleep under the same blanket
Dead we use the same coffin; won't we be one in all?

Poetry cuts through the restrictive layers that smother the soul. The Chinese have sensible souls. Illusions come and go, brought about by cosmic imbalance—the sky clouds up and clears again.

Van Gulik's studies always refer to the China of the past, within the era of forty centuries that preceded the so-called democracies of Sun Yat-sen and Chiang Kai-shek; well before Mao Tse-tung's attempts at absolute communism, now tempered by pragmatism. Van Gulik, interviewed by a journalist of one of Holland's more prestigious newspapers, said, after returning from a visit to Communist China in 1964:

"There are certain basic Chinese traits that will never change, and some of them have always been compatible within communism. Mere capitalism, in the sense of greedily going for profit only, has been looked down upon since earliest recorded times. The Chinese favor equal opportunities for all their citizens, and vital industries have always been owned by the state."

The erudite ambassador then tells us that the Chinese will try out anything to see if, either as a whole or in parts, it may be of use to them, and will ruthlessly discard whatever they may not care for, without bothering to over-criticize the offensive subjects afterwards. The experiments may take a while, like with communism now, and with the teachings of Confucius in the past.

Written law does not always reflect reality, and even when the female aspect was blamed for anything that went wrong, attitudes could be found that pointed in the opposite direction. Van Gulik, in another interview (1965) said:

"China had good books on birth control and the techniques of lovemaking long before the West began to count its years. After studying still available material I concluded that, then like now, the Chinese pay much respect to their sexual contacts. Disdaining the flesh has never been a popular creed. Bodily functions were always completely accepted and I don't believe that a figure like St. Paul could ever become a symbolic reality in the Chinese mind. Ever since 5000 years before Christ, the Orient considered sex to be a self-evident and healthy drive, in which the human being is not placed in the center. Both Chinese and Japanese thought sees the male/female relationship as a reflection of the cosmos. We merely move with the rhythm of nature, mirror sun and moon, earth and heaven, water and fire. This proves the equality of man and woman, an equality that has come to us from a far past. Man may appear to be prominent but is possessed by woman, like he possesses her. The Chinese have always been conscious of these important truths."

Again, the scholar speaks, carefully phrasing conclusions drawn from diligent studies, restrained by fact and dogma.

In *The Red Pavilion*, the most romantic and sensuous of the Judge Dee series, van Gulik the novelist shows us harsh reality, after a playful introduction. His descriptions of illness and decay don't ignore gruesome details. A foul smell wafts from the pages and, while we debate whether we want to be put off even further, he drags us along, and successfully proves that human love can free us from the rot of old age. Provided, of course, *"love risks all and everything—wealth, reputation, future, no matter what. That it will reject anything in total indifference, preferring only the beloved."*

In which case the poor hovel that shields the lovers becomes more beautiful than a palace, and the embrace of leper and blind toothless whore (once a famous statesman and a lovely court lady, who loved each other then but were separated by fate) a subtle insight that we behold with rare pleasure.

Separated from you,
what is left to me to offer?
No more than this poem,
stained by clear tears.

An artistic statement, by Yü Hsüan-chi, ninth century, a free woman who disliked stereotyped ideas. She inspired van Gulik into creating the essential attractive learned and conceited female whom he describes as the poetess in *Poets and Murder*.

10

Judge Dee is wary of the fetid corruption that frequently occurs in both Buddhism and Taoism, and fascinated by the mysterious freedom centered in both thought systems alike. Buddhist and Taoist principles are demonstrated in all the Judge Dee books, although not always defined for the reader. Naturally these themes must originate in the author's scholarly studies. Van Gulik dedicated two of his more 'serious' works to his favorite musical instrument, the *qin** or Chinese lute: *The Lore of the Chinese Lute* (Tokyo, 1940) and *Hsi K'ang and His Poetical Essay on the Lute* (Tokyo, 1941). Within these learned dissertations we might perhaps find opportunities to analyze some of the author's reflections.**

First of all, what's so special about the *qin*?

"Its beauty," van Gulik tells us, *lies not so much in the succession of notes as in each separate note itself. The timbre is of utmost importance, there are very great possibilities of modifying the colouring of one and the same tone . . .*

---

*Ch'in in the Wade-Giles system.
**My copies were found by Asian Rare Books, New York.

Van Gulik with a *qin* master, Chungking (ca. 1945)

*The techniques by which these variations in timbre are ef-
fected is extremely complicated: of the vibrato alone there
exist no less than 26 variations."* There's more information in this vein. The tune hardly counts, it's the abstract
sound that transports us. Or not 'us' so much. Not just
anybody can play this subtle instrument, capable of making us float into the void. The Chinese doctors of literature, the exclusive Ph.D.'s of antiquity, the magistrates
and court officials who ruled the land, had claimed the
lute for their higher levels. (One is not surprised to read,
in other studies, that a lot of *qin*s were smashed during
the Cultural Revolution). There is a photograph of Dr.
van Gulik in Chungking, 1945. He's listening to a *qin*
master playing. Incense smoulders, the master wears a
Taoist hat, two Chinese disciples in white frocks concentrate in awe. This is not a performance but a ritual, and
van Gulik seems very straight, very attentive, most
taken in by the whole thing. If percussion instruments
such as drums, clappers and gongs are associated with
Buddhist meditation then the seven stringed lute must
be the Taoist vehicle, that takes the disciple out of his
self-inflicted limitations. These books were written when
WW II was on. The Netherlands were already occupied
by Nazi forces. Another form of Fascism pushed Japan
into the turmoil. Van Gulik played the lute. He was
happy. Not silly happy, but at positive mental peace, in
his study that he was about to lose, together with his first
extensive art collection and library. He would lose his
valuable lute, too, but he found another in China. What
sort of instrument?

It's a 'zither,' unfretted, with a soundbox composed of two
boards. The upperboard is concave and made of softwood,
the bottom board is flat and made of hard wood. Seven

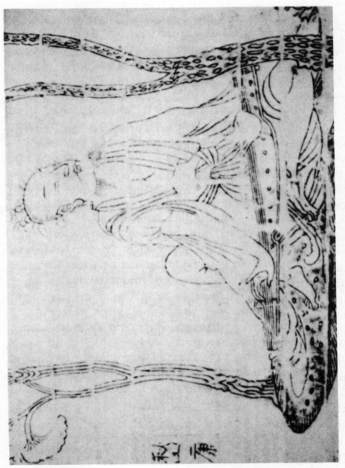

Hsi K'ang and his *qin*

silk strings (some lutes have five, others nine strings, but
the seven stringed instrument is considered to be proper) are strung over the soundbox, and the bottom board
of same has two rectangular perforations, called the
'dragon pond' and the 'phoenix pool.' As the lute is a quiet
instrument it usually needs a second soundbox; the table
it is put on. The modern wooden table has a hollow com-
partment.

The instrument of a sage. Hsi K'ang was such a Taoist
recluse, legend has it. He played the lute and was the
saintly musician of a group of seven sages, who met in a
bamboo grove. Hsi K'ang wrote an essay on the use of the
lute and van Gulik wrote an essay on the essay. In the
preface we hear that his translation of Hsi K'ang's final
rumination (Hsi was executed shortly after setting down
his thoughts) might not be accurate. *"The text offers a few
knotty passages,"* van Gulik says. He wishes that there
would be other more qualified scholars who might be able
to do a better job, provided that, *"they would have a certain familiarity with the lute, which perhaps they had no
opportunity to acquire."* Now it so happened that van Gulik did have the skill to play this most rare of instruments and therefore felt that he was qualified to enter
the mind of a Taoist adept.

But there were seven supreme Taoists, meeting in the
bamboo grove, in the third century. They were regarded
as ideal recluses and the Pleiad became a well known
motif, still used today, shown on pottery and paintings.
The venerable gentlemen play chess, write poetry, drink
wine, but Hsi K'ang always plays the lute. They are in
complete harmony with the cosmos. They keep cool under
rustling leaves. They are a legend.

Legends, however, are usually provably untrue. They

embody a thought, an ideal scene, and translate badly into regular life. What really went on with the seven holy men? Van Gulik's study shows that they weren't holy and they didn't live in a bamboo grove. They were rich and important, powerful court officials, not in the beginning so much when they were still idealistic, but slowly their environment corrupted them. Their meetings became infrequent, then stopped. There was one exception, Hsi K'ang. Like Socrates he was incorruptible, and like Socrates he was condemned to death. He played the lute before the execution and died in peace.

Was Hsi K'ang's immortal spirit saved because of his lute?

We might look at the idea of 'immortality' here. Being free of death stands for being free of dualism, to be beyond mind and matter, spirit and soul. Taoist magic desperately searched for a literal solution. There might be an elixir of life that can be brewed in a cauldron, or stalagtites are eaten for they 'freeze' the mind, leading to hallucinations where time is of no importance. Sexual functions can be perverted perhaps into an exercise that will prolong mere physical life. Certain breathing exercises become all important. Some sages jog. Anything so as to avoid dying. However, actual death does matter to the prospective immortal, and shows up in relevant literature. *"When Hsi K'ang was about to be executed on the eastern market of Lo-yang, the capital of Wei, he was entirely unperturbed. Drawing his lute unto him he pulled the strings. When he had finished the melody he said,* 'my brother-in-law asked me to teach him this tune, but I persistently refused. The melody now dies with me.' We hear he played something called "Great Peace." The audience was moved.

A study by J.C.Y. Watt, published in the magazine

Orientations (November 1981, an issue dedicated to the memory of Dr. van Gulik), tells us that the seven stringed lute had become a holy instrument indeed. Duke Ping (sixth century B.C.) got into deep trouble because he insisted on listening to *qin* music before being morally worthy of the experience. Marquis Wen (426–387 B.C.) dared to dance to the lute and was severely criticized. The music attracted the holy bird, the crane, who would rightfully dance to it, and every scholar who searched for supreme harmony had a seven stringed lute on his wall, whether he could play it or not. Court musicians had to learn to play the magic instrument, and one of the most glorious Chinese compositions ever, *Water and Clouds on the Rivers Xiao and Xiang,* was specially composed for the superb zither.

Gradually the lute became part, perhaps even the essence, of what in high circles was supposed to be mystic joy. *Qin* players even show up in modern paintings, and the setting, although perhaps different in style, is still basically the same. The scene is what van Gulik himself would draw later in his life: the lone hermit at peace in his cabin. All he now owns are some books, and his only furniture is a shelf to hold them. A crane struts next to him when he walks. He plays the lute when the weather forces him indoors, on his special simple table, or on his knees when he can go outside. His own music takes him away, on the wings of the crane, out of earthly dust and dirt. The setting is of extreme simplicity and elegance.

And of extreme continuous impossibility. The Taoist Hsi K'ang was a rich man who enjoyed the bodily comforts. If he did spend a day off in his cabin he would take his laundry home to his wife.

Still, the idealized simplicity may very well exist,

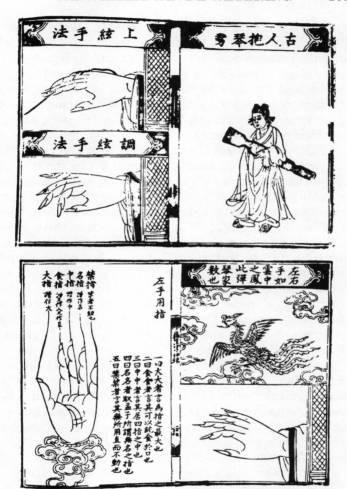

Pages from a *Qin* handbook, the *Fengxuan Xuanpin*, published in 1540

within an immortality that is to come to all of us, that,
Taoism claims, is with us already. The blissful feeling of
ultimate freedom does occur, when we suddenly no longer
worry about responsibilities and possessions, death creep-
ing up, and the trouble on TV. "This," is what we want
the sage to say, while he plucks on a string, causing one
of the twenty-six vibratos, "is the true everlasting happiness that we have earned."

So the Seven Sages of the Bamboo Grove were not all
that wise, and the anecdotal material (as in the case of
Judge Dee) has crowded out most of the historical facts.
In reality they didn't restrict themselves to simplicity,
but combined maximal salaries with minimal duties. One
of them, Liu Ling (221–300) turned into a pathetic alco-
holic, followed by a page who filled him up from a jar.
Shan T'ao turned traitor and helped to bring the group's
only true hero, the lute player Hsi K'ang, to his death on
a false charge. Shan T'ao also became a henchman of the
cruel dictator Generalissimo Ssû-ma Chao, and lived a
life of extreme and evil luxury, claiming that he had
spent twenty years roaming through hills and valleys,
while he 'realized his Tao.'

One out of seven—not a bad percentage for achieving
immortality on this lowly planet. Hsi K'ang practised the
Taoist art well, learned how to achieve excellence in complete detachment, and encouraged a Dutch Sinologue so
that he could pass on his joy to us. The means here is a
certain type of music, which, as the sage says: *is a vehicle
for guiding and nurturing the spirit, and for elevating
and harmonizing the emotions.*

Then there are some hints as to how to play: *The open-
ing bars of a lute melody are strong like lofty mountains,
or again they resemble heaving waves: broad and generous,*

Judge Dee reading in his library

majestic and imposing . . . One must shun specious ef-
fects, and concentrate on one's play, abiding by the rules,
playing on quietly. Then the tones shall be imposing and
expressive. Distinctly and clearly they end, and finally the
coda in 'floating tones' echoes faintly the main motif of the
melody.

That's nice, but there is also some arrogance hidden
here. Hsi K'ang only speaks to a small circle of his peers. By
claiming the lute as strictly reserved for the upper class, the
Taoist mandarins implied that only those who, like themselves, were capable of lofty thoughts could play refined music, destined to bring them to even greater heights. They, as
Professor Watts points out, confused theory with practice,
and many an acclaimed *qin* 'master' of today is only capable
of producing sweet and seductive notes, so abstracted that
they can no longer claim meaning.

This would not apply to two exemplary practitioners of
the rare instrument, Robert van Gulik himself and Magistrate Dee. Please check the illustration. The old wood-
cut shows the historical Judge Ti Jen-chieh (Dee's full
name) in his study, and the instrument on his desk (half
wrapped in its cover) is one of the means that has helped
to shape his brilliant mind.

11

Mandarins, gentleman scholars, preferred intellectual and artistic byways to the main thoroughfares of issues that were supposed to matter so much. We therefore may, perhaps, be excused if we associate the mandarin approach with gentility, and picture, perhaps, a kind old man harmlessly engaged in some trivial study.

We could, perhaps, be wrong.

The Dutch scholarly magazine *China*, published quarterly before WW II, contained an introductory chapter of van Gulik's book *Kuei-ku-tzû, the Philosopher of the Ghost Vale,* in the May 1939 issue.

Although I should have known better, I expected, when I stumbled across the essay, that it would offer another entry to van Gulik's curiosity aimed at the bizarre—and in so far I was right. But the thoughts offered here are more than reflections of mildly noteworthy facts dug up from a far and obsolete past.

Kuei-ku-tzû lived during the period of the 'Warring States' (5th to 3rd century B.C.) and was one of the then abundant wandering philosophers and therapeutic psychologists 'who taught wisdom to make a living.' His name came down to us because he managed to attract the ire of both 'unworldly' Buddhism and the moral 'down-to-earth' ideals of Confucius, the unbudgeable arch-fundamentalist of Chinese thought and behavior. Only detached and adventurous Taoism accepted Kuei's most unusual solutions and even incorporated the rebel sage's teachings into its elusive canon.

Kuei's thinking pivoted around the best possibility for worthwhile human rule, rejecting all theories aimed at pleasing common minds.

Confucius insisted that all governing should be concerned with the people's welfare, while the Chinese Legalist School, like Fascism and Communism today, advocated total obedience to an absolute system in which only rulers' wishes, rather than the needs of the ruled, can be granted. This dual choice had, up till then, not been extended, but Kuei-ku-tzû, a simple but reputedly enlightened ambulant teacher, smashed easily through, proposing a third way out in which political situations can be brought about in a most optimal manner.

Our obscure philosopher, whose ancient book—a set of damaged bamboo strips bound by silk cords, battered and incomplete—is being brought back to life again, begs to think differently *in essence*. Kuei recommends a rule effected neither by the people nor by self-maddened pathological dictators cooked up in the soup that spawned Hitler and Pinochet, but by a new model of leader, that Kuei then sets out to describe in detail.

Kuei's type of Superior Man may remind us of Nietzsche's *Ubermensch* or the 'sly man' held up as example in the writings of Gurdjieff and Ouspensky. Neither king by birth, nor president elected, the ideal executive places himself in total charge 'simply by the virtue of his own ability.' Beyond morals, uncannily intelligent, gifted both in pragmatic science and the realm of abstract thought, we meet an exception to what is known as 'the small circle of necessity' who does not need to strut about on the governmental stage from which he frightens his people. What is this magnificent man's motivation? No more than *his will to rule.*

Kuei-ku-tzû's treatise has thought of all the possibilities. How does this new brand of Superior Man (who lacks most of the redeeming qualities inspired by Confucian morality) manage to settle himself on the highest perch? Either, Kuei says, constitutionally or not.

Preferably Superman, Kuei advises, should rule through a weak Prince whom he reduces to a puppet whose strings he can manipulate without strenuous effort, but should the legal ruler prove to be hard to handle in any way—away with the numbskull, and Superman seizes the throne and declares himself King of all the lands.

No morals. Please. This superman is a free man, a Taoist sage, out of reach of grabbing human hands, and of divine grabbing hands that human wishful thought projects.

There's much shrewd advice, Dr. van Gulik tells us with obvious pleasure and anticipation, that Kuei offers in his illuminating treatise.

What to do in order to change ourselves into a Supreme Being is mostly concerned, Kuei lectures, with using men in the way they happen to present themselves to us. Don't worry about trying to educate or improve their quality, Kuei implores. Unevolved folks are far too stubborn to fulfill their potential, but all of them have useful sides to their characters, special talents, that they will offer us gladly so that we may use them in any way that might please our own interests.

Does this Minister of State happen to be a good fellow, concerned about taking care of our subjects? Splendid. Don't bother to bribe him or corrupt his pure mind in any way. Let him be unselfish and hard working to his limits so that the work gets done, and the state, which is the ego of the ruler, may be fed, cleaned, serviced, rested, kept healthy. The general has a big mouth in the capital? Promote him to Field Marshall and let him conquer all neighboring lands. He perishes and is covered with posthumous medals.

This Departmental Chief is a Wise Man? He understands the rhythms of reason? Walks the way? So let him walk all the ways of the land, and preach and lecture, for the state will benefit by proper rhythm. Bless the man and he will, wisely, bless his King.

Let all the ruled follow their talents and let Superman not interfere with their little ways. While cats catch mice, moles grub in dark tunnels for a living, vultures feast on carrion and lions stamp about and roar, while everybody is usefully employed, the true ruler enjoys his power leisurely, in most luxurious and tasteful surroundings.

Van Gulik apologizes throughout the article for his fascination with the cynical Kuei's teachings. Kuei-ku-tzû himself isn't a good example of his own glorious creed. No ruler would hire the positive philosopher and he had to beg for a living. Theory and practise don't always harmonize in a single man's life. Even so, his small book has been well studied throughout the more than two thousand years that followed its private publication. Officially frowned upon by Chinese rulers, Kuei's practical hints have been followed both throughout imperial and communist rule. Be not fooled, van Gulik warns—this subtle thought is not another form of mere opportunism. Kuei's book comes in three parts, the first two sections teach us how to change others into our tools. That the tools may be as good as they can be, will, Kuei exhorts, be brought about by carefully observing our present and future servants, so that we can analyze their behavior. Are they happy? Make them happier and see what they do when they're drunk with joy. Depressed? Make life a little harder. Now what do they do? We'll determine their limits, read their hidden thoughts.

But then, in Kuei's third lecture, we're taught how to know and manipulate *ourselves.* A proper study of this exotic literary jewel that van Gulik praised and presented in several tactful ways, will make it impossible for the ruler to misbehave. His consequent and pure selfishness will, ultimately, serve *all* selves.

Van Gulik also considers the work as 'religious'—part of the teaching of Taoist *Wu-wei,* the art of 'doing nothing,' where we learn to move and advance with the power of our male Yang, while the female dark and moist Yin allows us to hide and rest. Van Gulik also mentions the identical natures of all opposites, shows how Yang in its extreme form manages, uproariously, to change into the most quiet and fertile form of Yin. *'Yang seeks Yin, and from it borrows its power. Yin eternally strives after a connection with Yang, always borrows Yang's abundant energy.'*

Van Gulik offers his lucky find, and interpretation, for what they may be worth to the reader, defining Kuei's words as *'solid common sense that, through the ages, sustained the Chinese people.'* And should the reader wish to destroy Kuei's 'cynicism' by total rejection, then he may still, hopefully, admire the audacity of this most courageous antique hermit, wandering by the wayside.

The article on the Sage of the Ghost Vale only appeared

once and was intended to be a teaser for an actual book in which van Gulik presents the full text (as available, for the original work only survives in part) of Kuei's thesis, plus ample commentary of course, and a complete treatment of criticisms by acknowledged Chinese scholarly sources.

Alas, the manuscript disappeared on the way to a Shanghai printer, in 1939, during the troubles of the Chinese-Japanese war. Van Gulik, while fleeing Japan, subsequently lost his own notes as well, and gave up on the entire project. All that survives is twelve pages of small print and one not too clear illustration, but the article, nevertheless, contains enough tempting material to inspire us to continue a quest aimed at insight and both amusing and sustaining adventure.

12

Van Gulik's fascination with Taoism, in its 'Tricks or Treats' aspect, comes up again in 1954, when he publishes a lengthy article entitled *"The Mango Trick in China,"* subtitled *An Essay on Taoist Magic*, and issued as part of the scholarly magazine *Transactions of the Asiatic Society of Japan, third series*. The 58 page dissertation exhaustively analyzes a Chinese phenomenon that probably had its origins in India. The trick has to do with magic growth and works equally well with mangos, peonies, pears and other organic matter. Growing fruit from pips is reduced to a matter of minutes, while the magician mutters his mantras and the public gapes. Impossible, yet demonstrable truth—as the pip is buried, covered with a cloth. Remove the cloth and there's the seedling; again, there's the bush or tree; again, there's the fruit; again, the fruit is ripe and can be eaten, or the flower can be cut, taken home, put in vase.

Like the rope trick (where the magician climbs a rope he throws into the air) the public is bamboozled by a form of hypnotism or suggestion.

Taoism is a religion and the purpose of any religion is

to 're,' *again,* 'ligare,' *join.* With what? With heaven, gods, God, our deepest being, our true purpose, our lost happiness. As heaven, gods or God are invariably involved, we deal with matters far beyond mere comprehension, so any wondrous trick could be in order.

Since earliest times, and Chinese civilization goes back 4000 years, forms of Taoist alchemy were known in China. Priests searched for the elixir of life, mixed lead and cinnabar, futilely tried to manufacture gold, picking up acceptable and workable knowledge while conning the public, that stared at them 'with their eyes confused and their pupils astray.' Taoists sometimes even joined up with their competitors, the Buddhists, mixing legitimate curiosity as to the ultimate causes of the creation in general, and themselves in particular, with an urge to make money from the multitude, and have a good time. Van Gulik's seemingly dry studies (the treatise is no Judge Dee tale, ostensibly offered to amuse) provide such juicy information as that the 'sumptuous nunnery,' Yung-ning-szu, fifth century, was really a funfair, sponsored by an emperor's son, where elaborate feasts were served by luscious dancing girls. When the prince died, his brother, a 'sexual pervert,' took over and the temple became even jollier and finally functioned as a circus. Erotic acts were interspersed with juggling and tricks, such as melons and dates that grew in a few moments from pips.

Exotic monasteries flourished and some, especially those of the Northern Buddhist school, added classes in which the student priests were taught how to create mass suggestion and what to do to bring about optical illusion.

What is van Gulik doing? Replacing our answer-seeking wonder by cynical disbelief?

Not at all. He works as a true scientist, as an intelligent observer, and attempts to explain what is really going on. In the West the saints have been marching in for thousands of years, too, and serve as a focus for our deeper, subconscious thought. A previous chapter mentioned the Seven Sages of the Bamboo Grove, and van Gulik now introduces a group of eight earlier immortals, originating in a hazy but fascinating past. A Confucianist scholar of the T'ang period (the time of Dee), a certain Han Yü (768–824), is an uncle of one of the eight immortals. This nephew, master Han Hsiang, steps out of the legend and shows himself as a trickster. Confucianism, being a set of moral rules, and Taoism, being high mysticism, are constantly at war and we might suppose that the practical Chinese would prefer to side with definable goodness, but van Gulik's inquiry proves differently, again.

Before we get into the actual story a brief introduction of the eight immortals will supply us with a set of interesting archetypes. Number 1 is a fat fellow who shows his contempt for the prim and proper by not wearing a hat, and slopping about in a loose gown that leaves his ample breast and belly bare. He's an important gent, however, and the arrogance of his vast bulk tells us not to try and push him over. Number 2, another free lance artist, is shown as a percussionist (carrying drums and clappers) riding his mule backwards. Number 3, the patron saint of fortunetellers, again demonstrates his Taoist disdain by not wearing a hat, while playing an immortal tune on his flute or nibbling on a peach, the juice of which is identical to the eternal elixir. Number 4 is more subtle, for he shows himself as a crippled old beggar, hungry and dressed in rags, who doesn't wear a hat out of rudeness but because he can't afford its price. He is testing our faith for he is no one less than the saint of medicine, who, if we treat him respectfully, will cure all ills. Number 5, the arch-musician, is not performing right now, but studies a map of yin and yang while, well dressed and impressive, he rests a moment on a fallen tree in the forest. Number 6 is very interesting, for his dignified shape leans on a domesticated devil. Here, surely, we have Jung's 'individuated man,' or the 'superior man' who answers our questions in oriental oracle books, or the 'sly man' propagated by the Armenian sage Gurdjieff. The subconscious has come out in the open and no longer threatens but supports. If this immortal had killed his devil the demon wouldn't be helping him out. This saintly Taoist is no less than the patron of all barbers (the surgeons of antiquity) and devil banners (ancient incarnations of today's psychiatrists, clinical psychologists, psychotherapists and their ilk). Our hero does have to wear a sword, to discipline the more forceful ogres, and a flywhisk, to swat the little fellows if they get too bold. Number 7 is a girl-saint, showing by her odd habits (one foot shod, one bare, trailing a string of loose cash through the dust) that she is well away from all 'acceptable' levels. She carries some musical instrument (usually a flute) and a basket filled with flowers, and inspires both musicians and all Chinese florists. Then there is Number 8, another female beauty displaying a large lotus flower and an immortal fruit. She also plays the flute and vaguely represents harmonious households. Endless stories are told about these exalted representations of the deeper levels of our minds, and the 8 Immortals are shown in paintings, sculptures, decorations of household articles and simple cartoons. Music is dedicated to them and they are central characters in poems. Their images differ significantly, depending on the talents and insights of the artists, but they all perform tricks, 'confusing our eyes and twisting our pupils astray.' They're also often drunk, but not on poisonous alcohol that degenerates the mind, but on the pure, liberating herbal drugs taken from heavenly gardens. One of them, Number 3, is Han Hsiang.

In order to clearly show how the Chinese controversy between the practical and poetic parts of the human (Chinese) mind is set up, van Gulik painstakingly traces the legend of the immortal pseudo-evil Han-hsiang-tzu and his pseudo-immortal good uncle Yü. We are given various versions, complete with sources and learned notes. The basic plot is as follows:

Uncle Yü is the model-man, who passed the imperial exams and in due course became a high official (like Judge Dee). There's nothing spectacular about him, except a perfectionist attitude toward toeing preset lines. Yü is such a perfect example of what (human) things should be like that he runs a school where he teaches future officials. Enters nephew Hsiang, who comes to the capital. Enrolled in uncle's school Han does very badly. He insults everyone, doesn't study and gets habitually drunk. Before kicking him out uncle Yü berates his relative. *"Can't you do anything right?"*

Nephew Hsiang now performs the 'mango trick' (but he does it with instant peonies). His uncle is dumbfounded, especially when his nephew tells him to read what's written on every petal of every instant-(from a pip)grown flower. In impressive handwriting the lines say: *The clouds obscure the pass, where could I find a home? The snow is too high for my horse to advance.*

Nephew Hsiang leaves.

Shortly thereafter the emperor, taken in by Buddhist

thought (Buddhism ranking about as high as Taoism in
lofty detachment and surrealist truth) wants a bone from
the Buddha's remains so as to have a focus for his medi-
tations. Uncle Yü, the orthodox teacher of all that is proper,
worries that the emperor has gone crazy. He politely says
so and is banished to a small town eight thousand *li*
away. During the trip he becomes stuck in a snowbound
mountain pass and laments loudly, when his nephew
steps from the fog and respectfully greets his learned uncle. Hsiang puts up Yü in a comfortable inn and there's a
long dialogue providing Hsiang's superior wisdom. Uncle
Yü gives up the narrowmindedness of mere morality and
opens his mind to higher truth. Later, as his nephew predicts, he is invited back to the court again. All ends well.

Van Gulik must have found these tales of wayward immortals helpful when he fantasized about being a hermit
in a cabin, overlooking the vast calm waters of Lake
Biwa, Japan. Perhaps the poem, written by Han Yü in
honor of his Taoist and most enlightened nephew, quoted
in Dr. van Gulik's treatise, was, in part, his own lament,
and solution:

Although I became a ranking official,
My meagre salary proved insufficient for my needs.
And see, what state have I come to now?
. . . .
The rain drips from my roof into the empty street.
In the morning I stay in bed, unable to rouse myself,
Thinking of my far-away home, I am full of sadness.
Then who is it who comes and knocks on my door?
On my inquiry the guest proves a member of my family.
He says that he possesses extraordinary abilities,
That he searches mysteries and knows the works of Heaven.

He exhorts me not to sorrow over things gone by,
And predicts that in the future I shall rise again.

So, perhaps, the scholar van Gulik here gives us a
hint, as on page 139 of the treatise. The Mango Trick is
only to dumbfound us, but once we become credulous, our
mental doors open up, so that we may be initiated into
the true mysteries, by the helpful relative, the projection
of this Chinese subconscious who tells us (page 143):

I can, in the space of one round of wine,
make flowers bloom that very instant.
Those who can follow me in my studies
Will contemplate with me the Immortal Flower.

At the Royal Netherlands Embassy, Tokyo, 1965

13

Dr. Robert Hans van Gulik died in September 1967. During May of that year he finished his last book, *The Gibbon in China*.

Gibbons (the word 'gibbon' was coined by Marco Polo, the first European to describe this exotic creature, who called it *gibbone*, meaning 'hunchback') were van Gulik's best friends. He had kept monkeys since his youth and anybody who ever interviewed him mentions this unusual company. In The Hague, in van Gulik's stately official residence at the Hovestraat, capuchin monkeys gamboled about, climbed his bookcases, swung from his art treasures, even fingered his calligraphy. He couldn't keep gibbons there, for these superior beings do not take to the Dutch moist and drafty climate, and lack of space. They thrived, however, in his oriental homes with their high ceilings and open doors, with access to spacious gardens and tall trees. Of all the gibbons van Gulik was close to, the Malaysian Bubu was his most cherished companion, and he even dedicated a book to her, in which the hero is a gibbon.

The Dutch government traditionally commissions an

貢余因檢故事凡打捕剑皆南鄉人遂召南鄉村老諸人告之眾唯而去旬餘日老一人來告云家捕猿之命已號召得三百餘夫合圍得一小黑猿於獨嶺上二日夜矣乞批帖督隋村益夫二百盡伐嶺木則猿可復余遂如其請三數日异一臂猿至予驗其形似皆如簡冊所云但無通臂者為之說恐別有種復詢諸土人云惟臂長者為之猿其類難非一皆短臂蒼毛者烏得長臂之猿而雄至何謨如此又有人云猿初生與智囊卽轉黑為雌遂與黑為孕余未深信與數書而轉黑為色轉黑為黃漬去其藝深信與智年遇轉黑為異熏後知雄與囊漸潰去乃固然者方釋其疑又諸簡冊所不載猿善攀木以黑者交以為此又慈乎五百人以旬日伐援跳躍迅捷乃能致之毋蒸乎五百人以旬日之勞僅得其一也又剙象鄧指頂家惟頂上普有山子人獲一猿來献面黑身白惟頂上普有

黑毛如指闊一縷直至脊盡處有人云猿初生時黑至百餘歲漸成黃而為雌又數百歲方變為白其有黑毛日頂貫脊有又異然則唐人之詩有云黃猿領白兒亦謨矣初生之兒登有白者余遂攜畜之三數年罷馴戀忽疾作而斃瘞小橫山側與鶴冢甚馴戀忽疾作而斃瘞小橫山側與鶴冢枏並

⑯又天保縣令送一黑猿來繫於爐有閂子黲之相距尚七八尺忽其右臂引而長遂挺門子之衣幾為所製而猿之左肩則已無臂乃知猿党不為兩所狎終日默坐

通臂猿也此猿覺日近餓死與之食不顧斃

丁未春荷蘭高羅佩釟
於東京使署之尊明閤

An example of van Gulik's Chinese text from *The Gibbon* in China

author to write the 'book of the year' that is then presented, during the first week of April, to anyone who spends some money in a bookstore. Van Gulik wrote the 1962 issue, a novelette called *Four Fingers*, perhaps his best tale ever, and had it inscribed to *"My faithful companion, the gibbon Bubu, deceased and buried in Malaysia, July 12, 1962."*

A simian sharing a literary honor with homo sapiens, understandable, for van Gulik did get irritated by the members of his own species. He was heard to say, on several occasions: *"I allow my monkeys to go where they please. Animals are decent chaps, they never abuse a situation."*

In *Four Fingers* a fictional gibbon provides an important clue, but van Gulik's last work is a scholarly effort. Aware of the serious nature of the disease that was about to kill his body he was in a hurry and had the book photocopied from his manuscript, rather than typeset. This unique solution provides us with the opportunity to see how impeccably he worked, both with the typewriter and his brush. The Chinese text especially is a joy for the eye, as are the miniature illustrations that introduce and divide his chapters and sections.

A gibbon is a primate, a link between the animal kingdom and our own realm, and shares its noteworthy niche with chimps, orangutangs and gorillas. Gibbons, like the other primates, can walk on their hindlegs, have no tail, and like to reason. Unlike us they are fairly friendly and will not attack unless cornered or unusually frightened. Only chimps and gibbons can share our homes. Orangutangs and gorillas are too strong, their friendly hugs are likely to kill us.

The gibbon is the only Chinese primate, a fact not generally noted until van Gulik's curiosity discovered their purview. The Chinese themselves were aware of the gracious animal's presence within their vast lands, and signal its peculiarities in their literature. Van Gulik quotes biologists and poets throughout his treatise.

There are many comments on their chanting. Gibbons habitually sing, early in the morning when the light is born, and in the evening, when the light dies out. Van Gulik was impressed by the musicality of their songs, and learned their chants himself. The poetry of the gibbons' being impressed him too, and the book reflects on the difference between the gibbons' high level of perception compared to the low practicality of lesser monkeys. The other Chinese member of the race, the macaque, does not sing, for he's too busy looking out for himself. The Chinese remarked on the macaque's restlessness and made the monkey a symbol of the human's superficiality, sudden inexplicable mood changes and even the human compulsion to steal. There's something intrinsically silly about the macaque, something truly human, and Chinese writers made, and make, grateful use of the similarity. The already mentioned macaque who features in the Chinese classical novel, available in the West as *Monkey* or *The Journey to the West*, symbolizes human intelligence. The part of our mind that fantasizes and conjures can get to heaven easily enough, in daydreams. So can dear Monkey, but he can't maintain his effort, so he is thrown out, for stealing plums and ravishing maidens. He has learned something, however, and remembers the way, and as the Sage's first disciple serves as guide. The macaque is egotistic, and therefore in continuous trouble, like Monkey in the book. Had he been a gibbon he would have had a much easier time, and saved much pain and suffering to the poor Sage, his master.

"The Gibbon," van Gulik writes, *"was the traditional pure-Chinese symbol of the poet and the philosopher, and of the mysterious connection between man and nature. The gibbon teaches man how he may make use of science and magic, and his morning and evening songs deepen poets' and painter's inspirations, in the dawn's mist and at night when there's a full moon."*

There are wolves and there are werewolves, but all gibbons are were-gibbons. The werewolf frightens, the were-gibbons inspire. Gibbons are airy apparitions, who prefer not to touch the ground and usually dangle from their disproportionately long arms, or swing quietly between very high branches. A male gibbon of the Chinese siamang species is only a foot and a half tall, but when he spreads his arms there's four feet between his fingertips. In order to keep their arms from dragging, they hold them above their heads when circumstances force them to come down to ground level. Their magic, van Gulik points out, is of such a high order that they always sat on his high cupboards, quite unlike the shrewd macaque who prefers to scurry underneath, to hide. The palms of a gibbon's hands and the soles of his feet show the same linear patterns as those of humans. A gibbon lives like a (decent) human being, with the same wife and just a few kids, and doesn't like to become too intimate with too many friends. The strongest gibbon serves himself last and all gibbons like properly ripened fruit, that they pick daintily and peel neatly.

One does not expect to be emotionally touched by a scholarly dissertation but I had a Moment visualizing an older high official, withdrawn and quiet, harmonizing with evolved spirits of a quite different order, who helped him lose his loneliness and share their solitude. On a

Van Gulik 'mumbling' with friend

photograph in one of the files I saw van Gulik 'mumbling' with Cheenee, a five year old male gibbon of the *hylobates agilis* genus. Cheenee has pushed out his lower jaw, keeps his lips tightly closed and frowns diligently. Van Gulik does likewise. They mumble together, as a preface, a warming up, toward the song of that evening. The gibbons' chant is a serious ritual that can only take place under certain conditions and in a hallowed place, usually at the top of a tree that the gibbon has tried out in various ways. If the view and everything else is right the gibbon will squat, spread its long arms, hold on tight and start a first stanza, repeating it softly until the sounds are rounded out well. When he has warmed up properly the true chant will follow, from low notes to high and with the volume increasing slowly. *WU-U-U-uuuuu,* while he shakes branches and extends his chest. He'll take the song back slowly afterward, gradually closing his mouth until he finishes in a musical extended groan. The final strophe is again a mumble. This process will be repeated dozens of times, and if there is any rude disturbance, like a car honking or some other animal piping up, he'll interrupt himself and relapse into an angry silence that will last for minutes, until he'll try again.

Gibbons are quiet between morning and evening chants but they do talk and hum a little. There's a proper language that van Gulik, of course, learned to speak fluently. *'Wok-wok?'* means *now what?* Or *you seriously intend this as a gift for little me? 'Ee-ee-eeeh'* means *Oh, hello! How very nice indeed to see you. Where have you been all this time?,* uttered only when the gibbon meets another gibbon whom he dearly loves, or a human being he has learned to trust.

Gibbons have a proper sense of proportion. They show more respect to a butler than to a gardener and prefer officers to soldiers, as van Gulik learned when his house caught fire and a dozen soldiers commanded by a lieutenant came to put out the flames. The gibbons kept pointing out danger spots to the officer in charge. Gibbons like to behave appropriately: when they investigate an object they study it gently from all sides, and don't tear it apart like a macaque would do. Gibbons like to use a toilet and some remember to flush the bowl.

Through the ages they have inspired subtle and artistic minds—

Morning after morning I contemplate clouds that sail along
Evening after evening I listen to the gibbons' chants
(the poet Shen Yüeh, 441–513)

The Wu Mountains join each other, for several hundreds
of miles
The River Pa weaves curve upon curve
The flute's chant becomes louder, dies away
The gibbons break their song and start all over again
(the emperor Chien-wên, 503–551)

When I hear the gibbons busying themselves in the pines
my intestines cramp, and I keep listening, counting my
tears, pair by pair
(crown prince Hsiao Tung, 501–531)

Van Gulik's soul must have stirred when he observed his advanced and cultured friends exercising around his mansions, but he didn't refer to them in a poem. He no

longer engaged in poetry, he said, in an interview with a
Dutch paper in 1964:

"As a student I did publish poems in Elseviers Monthly
Magazine. *They paid me ten guilders a page, quite a siz-
able sum in those days. However, I eventually decided
that the medium wasn't for me. Once I saw what Chinese
poets could do I lost courage completely. Their work is so
pure and exact that I knew I could never even dare to imitate their efforts."*

But he did dare to tell tales, like the following story,
from *The Gibbon in China*, but much abridged by me:

Eighth century: Candidate Litt. Sun K'o roams through
the country after flunking his doctorate exams. Near
Lake Wei-wang he spots a large mansion and a passerby
tells him that Miss Yüan lives there. Sun knocks on the
front door but nobody opens up. A side door hasn't been
locked, Sun enters and sees a young lady in the court-
yard. She reminds him of 'a pearl, bathed in moonlight,'
and of 'a willow, slowly unveiled by the morning fog that
wafts away,' she has 'an orchid's tender charm and the
complete form of a jade sculpture.'

The girl sings:
Some I find attractive, like a glowing wine,
Others as tasteless as dried grass.
Only the azure mountains and the white clouds
know the feelings that I store in my soul.

An affair develops: the failed student and the graceful
young lady embrace. They even get married and the student is now rich, for the former Miss Yüan owns much
property. Her yang harmonizes with his yin and the
happy couple begets two sons. Their happiness lasts for
many years until Sun has to go on a journey and meets a

former friend who, after becoming a doctor of literature, studied Taoist tricks. Sun tells him how he met his present wife and what a happy life he leads.

The friend worries. He explains Taoist magic, calling himself a student-adept. He has noticed, by studying Sun's general behavior, that Sun is bewitched. The mere fact that Sun doesn't suspect his wife of being a witch proves that she is. Perfect beauty and charm? A steady character even when irritated or actually harassed? Such total mastery of the art of *wu-wei*, the technique of how to let things happen without becoming active oneself, . . . how could a regular human being be such a saint? Sun's wife has to be an evil spirit, a were-wolf or a were-fox. Sun will have to kill her.

"How could I ever manage killing her," asks Sun, "if she is that almighty?"

The friend knows how to help out. He lends Sun his magic sword, made by a holy man in a cave.

Sun takes the weapon home but doesn't dare to use it. He loves his wife and hides the murderous tool, but she finds it and shows it to him. "Haven't I been good to you? Why do you want to kill me?"

Sun bows deeply and she forgives him. She breaks the sword as easily as if it were a twig. Their togetherness continues and Sun, encouraged by his wife, goes back to school, passes his final examination and is appointed as a magistrate in a faraway city. He travels there with his wife and sons and the family spends the night in a temple. Gibbons chant in the trees that evening and his wife goes to have a look. Sun goes after her but the gibbons leave as soon as he shows.

She gets a brush and composes her farewell poem:

*Muddled by love I stubbornly refused to return to my
original shape
As a joke I had transformed into a human and almost got
lost.
It's better for me now to follow my companions to the
mountains,
And make my voice heard between the fog and the clouds.*

She drops the brush and kisses her children. She bows
to her spouse. She tears off her clothes and changes into
a slender gibbon.

Sun watches her until she disappears in the treetops.

Yüan is Chinese for 'gibbon' so the Chinese reader
may have anticipated the denouement from the story's
start.

Make-believe, you will say, a mere fairy tale, and you're
right of course, but haven't we all glanced at women of
such lovely strangeness that they have made us wonder?
Van Gulik may have looked at his own gibbon, Bubu,
when he reflected on the story of the mysterious Lady
Yüan. A human simian. And a simian human.

Cheenee, the male gibbon van Gulik liked to mumble
with, had the run of the Dutch embassy in Kuala Lumpur,
Malaysia—a happy little chap until he caught cold. Cheenee was issued plenty of rest and love but the doctor saw
no improvement. He diagnosed double pneumonia, in-
jected antibiotics, had the patient spoonfed on fruit juice,
but Cheenee's condition kept slipping. He only slept by
now, and the family gave up hope.

The van Gulik's were having tea in the garden when
they suddenly noticed Cheenee, dragging his gracious
feet—minute step followed by minute step—aiming for
the embassy's tallest palm tree. The family watched quietly

as the gibbon reached the tree, embraced its trunk, painfully pulled its small hurting body up.

Finally, seventy feet higher, swaying softly in the breeze, Cheenee found a comfortable spot, wrapped his long arms around his small knees, and waited, looking calmly into space.

"A dignified death," van Gulik says in his book, *"that rightfully may make us humans feel envy."*

14

Dr. van Gulik's untimely death was advertised in my newspaper, and I didn't think anyone would object to me attending the funeral.

It was a farewell like so many others, with solemn portly men in dark suits, and strangely hatted and quiet ladies. The silence was interrupted by harrumphs, whispers, a groan here and there. Familiar pink showed in the raised faces of the audience, and other, more exotic shades. The Queen had sent her representative, a martial official in a uniform that was hard to classify. A general perhaps? His hat was heavy with gold braid and he carried a cavalry sword and an officious but gentle smile. The last of the sabre tigers, I thought. I was glad the general could make it, for I remembered that one of van Gulik's forefathers was martial too, a high-ranking British officer by the name of Gollicke—sent across the Channel to command troops who would attack a common enemy, the Spanish oppressors who took over Western Europe.

I may have closed my eyes—speeches kept coming slowly and their monotonous rhythm made my mind float

on solemn words, but perception is sometimes height-
ened when the body nods off. A most realistic vision appeared, containing all the naked ladies van Gulik had
drawn when illustrating his Chinese murder tales. There
they were, holding hands and hiding their feet (for ladies'
bare feet could not be shown in ancient China, as they
were crippled, not a good sight to behold). Lovely ladies
nevertheless, vainly trying to seduce their mighty magistrate, but having more luck with his stalwart assistants.
Some intimate scenes showed up, starring quiet Chiao
Tai and boisterous Ma Joong. Embarrassed I looked away,
concentrating on the tall figure of Judge Dee himself,
standing alone on the stage, a handsome figure indeed
with his full beard, growing into the sideflaps of his official silk hat. His wide shoulders sloped slightly in the
brocade robe, that rustled while he breathed slowly and
deeply. His two lieutenants, now done with their erotic
interval, stepped forward, flanking the chief, resplendent
in their uniforms of full colonels of the Imperial Guard,
wide and muscular chests protected by polished coats of
mail, adorned by golden dragons, spitting fire. Tao Gan
stepped from the shadows, smiling wanly. Ex con-man of
genius, now all powerful secretary of the Supreme Court,
an official on the highest salary scale, but still in a simple
patched robe, and a hat shiny with age. The unassuming
man next to him? Of course, old sergeant Hoong, private
counselor to Dee, sedate, modest and wise, simply dressed
in a black gown and a little square cap.

I saw Dr. van Gulik himself, too, in a three piece suit
with ashes spilled on waistcoat and trousers. His dark
eyes glint mysteriously behind the 'little round glasses'
that he doesn't need anymore but hasn't taken off yet. He
listens politely, waiting for the final release from official

duties here below. I don't hear his dry little cough, he breathes as easily as Dee. The two bow briefly to each other. Did I see them wink?

And look, there are Bubu and Cheenee, swinging on the joists high above the stage, swaying from their impossibly long and slender arms, mumbling, preparing for their musical chant of welcome, but they'll have to wait a little yet, for a professor from the famous University of Leyden holds forth. He speaks well, I believe, I can't quite get the words, as I listen from afar, struggling to raise my eyelids just a little.

Mr. Hendriks walks up the aisle, accompanied by Captain Uyeda. Hendriks is tall and thin, bent in memory of hellish torture. He holds his dripping felt hat and his threadbare raincoat is wet through. As he moves by me I notice the fragrance of juniper gin. Uyeda smells of saké. With his bent legs, in army wrapping, thick spectacles on a short flat nose, his overbite, and the long samurai sword pulled along by his slight body, he could have stepped out of a WW II propaganda pamphlet, but he raises no hatred. I feel that the noose that strangled him was a gate and that Mount Fuji's eternal snow will melt for Uyeda too, while, like all of us, he struggles with the ten thousand things, raised so mysteriously from the eternal all-encompassing void. The Arab terrorists from *The Given Day* smile at me too, reciting the poetry of the Koran, and make room for masters Gourd and Crane Robe, transcending their audience's ignorance jointly. The speakers are silent now, a requiem is sung by a hidden chorus. All illusions fade away. Van Gulik nods at us, turns, slowly walks away; a door opens, closes—where has he gone?

Zen bum Loo appears, bows, dips his broom in a

bucket of paint. He throws his faultless calligraphy at the wall:

We all return from where we came:
Where the flame went to, when we snuffed out the candle.

The large characters shine triumphantly on the wall. The audience rises, expresses its sympathies to the bereaved.

"Not *the* end," a Buddhist priest is saying, "only an end. A little one. There are so many."

Bibliography

An English-Blackfoot Vocabulary Based on Material from the Southern Peigans by C.C. Uhlenbeck and R.H. van Gulik. Verhandelingen der Koninklijke Akademie van Wetenschappen to Amsterdam, Afdeling Letterkunde, N.R., deel XXIX, no. 4, (Amsterdam; 1930), 263 pp.

Urvaçī, een oud-Indisch toneelstuk van Kālidāsa, uit den oorspronkelijken tekst vertaald, en van een inleiding voorzien [Urvaçī, an ancient Indian play by Kālidāsa, translated from the original, with an introduction]. (The Hague, Adi Poestaka; 1932), 84 pp., with vignettes by van Gulik

A Blackfoot-English Vocabulary based on material from the Southern Peigans, by C.C. Uhlenbeck and R.H. van Gulik. Verhandelingen der Koninklijke Akademie van Wetenschappen to Amsterdam, Afdeling Letterkunde, N.R., deel XXXIII, no. 2 (Amsterdam; 1934), xii + 380 pp.

Hayagrīva, the mantrayānic aspect of horse-cult in China and Japan, with an introduction on horse-cult in India and Tibet (doctoral thesis, *cum laude*) (Leyden, Brill; 1935), x + 105 pp., illustrated

Mi Fu on ink stones; translated from the Chinese with an introduction and notes (Peking, Henry Vetch; 1938), xii + 72 pp., ills. and map.

The lore of the Chinese lute; an essay in Ch'in *ideology,* Monumenta Nipponica Monographs, vol. 3 (Tokyo, Sophia University; 1940), vi + 239 pp., illustrated

Hsi K'ang and his poetical essay on the lute, Monumenta Nipponica Monographs, vol. 4 (Tokyo, Sophia University; 1941) xvi + 91 pp., illustrated

Shukai-hen, a description of life in the Chinese factory at Nagasaki during the Ch'ien-lung period, translated from the original Chinese into Japanese, with a Japanese introduction and notes, in *Tōa ronsō* (Bunkyū-dō; Tokyo, 1941).

明末義僧東皐禪師集刊 *Tung-kao-ch'an-shih-chi-k'an* [Collected works of the Zen Master Tung-kao, a Monk Who Stayed Loyal to the Emperor during the End of the Ming], in Chinese, 149 pp with 3 pp in English. Printed for the author by Commercial Press (Chungking, 1944)

Dee Goong An, three murder cases solved by Judge Dee. An old Chinese detective novel translated from the original Chinese with an introduction and notes iv + iv + 237 pp. (Printed for the author by Toppan Printing Co., Tokyo; 1949).

春夢瑣言 *Ch'un Meng So Yen, Trifling Tale of a Spring Dream. A Ming erotic story, published on the basis of a manuscript preserved in Japan and introduced* (Tokyo, privately printed; 1950), 6 (English) + 19 (Chinese) pp.

Pi-hsi t'u-shuo 秘戲圖說, *Erotic colour prints of the Ming period, with an essay on Chinese sex life from the Han to the Ch'ing dynasty, B.C. 206—A.D. 1644* (Privately published in fifty copies, Tokyo, 1951),—3 volumes. I (English): xvi + 242 pp., 22 illustrations; II (Chinese) 秘書十種, 2 + 210 pp.; III (Chinese) 花營錦陣, 4 + 24 pp., 24 plates.

Ti Jen-chieh Ch'i-an, an historic novel [Chinese version of *The Chinese Maze Murders*]. Privately printed for the author, (Nan Yang Press, Singapore; 1953)

De boekillustraties in het Ming tijdperk [Book Illustrations in the Ming Period]. (The Hague, Nederlandse Vereniging voor druk-en boekkunst; 1955), 10 pp., 11 pp. of illustrations.

Siddam; an essay on the history of Sanskrit studies in China and Japan. Saravati—Vihara Series vol. 36 (Nagpur, International Academy of Indian Culture; 1956), 234 pp.

T'ang-yin pi-shih, 棠陰比事, *'Parallel cases from under the pear-tree,' a 13th century manual of jurisprudence and detection;* Sinica Leidensia vol. X (Leyden, Brill; 1956), xi + 198 pp.

Chinese pictorial art as viewed by the connoisseur. Notes on the means and methods of traditional Chinese connoisseurship of pictorial art, based upon a study of the art of mounting scrolls in China and Japan. Serie orientale 19 (Rome, Instituto Italiano per il Medio ed Estremo Oriente; 1958), 537 pp.

Lu Shih-hua, 陸時化 , *Scrapbook for Chinese collectors, A Chinese treatise on scrolls and forgers,* **Shu-hua shuo-ling** 書畫說鈴 , *translated with and introduction and notes* (Beirut, Imprimerie catholique; 1958), 84 pp. + 16 pp. Chinese text.

Sexual life in ancient China; a preliminary survey of Chinese sex and society from ca. 1500 B.C. till 1644 A.D. (Leyden, Brill; 1961), xvii + 392 pp., ills.

The Gibbon in China, an essay in Chinese animal lore (Leyden, Brill; 1967), 120 pp., illustrated, photographs, maps.

Articles

Contributions to the school paper *Rostra*, including poetry (some in French) and the essay "Van het schoone eiland" [From the beautiful isle], a reminiscence of the author's childhood on Java.

"Eenige opmerkingen omtrent de Shih Ching, het klassiekke Boek der Oden" [Some remarks concerning the *Shih-ching*, the classical Book of Odes], in *China* III (1928), pp. 133–147.

" 'Ku Shih Yuan'—De Bron der Oude Verzen" [*Ku-shih yüan*, the source of ancient verse], in *China* III (1928), pp. 243–269.

"De Bloeitijd der Lyriek" [The heyday of lyrical poetry], in *China* IV (1929), pp. 1229–143, 253–275; *China* V (1930), pp. 115–119.

"De mathematische conceptie bij de oude Chineezen" [The concept of mathematics among the ancient Chinese], in *Euclides, Nederlandsch Tijdschrift voor Wiskunde* (1929).

"Chineesche wonderverhalen" [Chinese tales of the supernatural], in *Tijdschrift voor Parapsychologie* I (1929), p. 158 sq. and p. 280 sq.; II (1930), p. 111 sq.

"De verwerkelijking van het onwerkelijke in het Chineesche schrift" [The realization of the unreal in the Chinese script], in *Elsevier's Geillustreerd Maandblad* LXXVII (1929), pp. 238–252, 318–333.

"Tsj'e Pie Foe, 'Het gedicht van den Rooden murr'" [*Ch'ihpi fu*, the poem of the Red Wall], in *China* V (1930), pp. 203–206.

"Oostersche schimmen" [Oriental shadows], in *Elsevier's Geillustreered Maandschrift* LXXXI (1931), pp. 94–110, 153–163; LXXXII (1932), pp. 230–247, 306–318, 382–389.

"De Wijsgeer Jang Tsjoe" [The philosopher Yang Chu], in *China* VI (1931), pp. 165–177; VII (1932), pp. 93–102.

"En nieuwe Fransche vertaling van Chineesche gedichten" [A new French translation of Chinese poetry, a critical review of G. Soulié de Morant, *Anthologie de l'amour chinois;* Paris, 1932], in *China* VII (1932), pp. 127–131.

Articles on Chinese history, language and literature in *Winkler Prins Encyclopedie*, 5th edition (Amsterdam; 1932–1938).

"De Wijze der Vijf Wilgen" [The Sage of the Five Willows—a discussion of the poet T'ao Yüan-ming], in *China* VIII (1933), pp. 4–27.

"In memoriam Henri Borel," in *China* VIII (1933), p. 167.

"Oude en nieuwe Chineesche oorlogszangen" [Chinese songs of war, ancient and modern], in *Chung Hwa Hui Tsa Chih, Orgaan van de Chineesche Vereeniging Chung Hwa Hui*, XI (1933), pp. 9–11.

"Henri Borel, 23 Nov. 1869—31 Aug. 1933," *idem*. XI, p. 68.

"Het Chineesche schaakspel" [Chinese chess], *idem* XI, pp. 99–105.

"Weerstand bieden; uit een artikel, geteekend Chün Ti, in de 'Shen-pao' van 21 Sept. 1933" [Resist; from an article in the *Shen-pao* of 21 Sept. 1933, signed Ch'ün Ti], in *idem* XI, pp. 145–146.

"De krijgsman die zijm eigen zoon offert. Een oud-Indisch verhaal, uit het Sanskrit vertaald en ingeleid" [The warrior who sacrifices his own son. An ancient Indian tale, translated from Sanskrit and introduced] in *idem* XII (1934), pp. 26–31.

"Chinese inkstones," in *idem* XII, pp. 79–83.

"De wijsgeerige archtergrond van de schilderkunst der Soeng-periode" [The philosophical background of the art of painting of the Sung-period], in *idem* XII, pp. 125–134.

"Chinese literary music and its introduction into Japan," in *18th Annals of the Nagasaki Higher Commercial School, part I (1937–1938) published in commemoration of Prof. Chōzō Mutō* (Nagasaki; 1937), pp. 123–160.

"Necrologie, Simon Hartwich Schaank," in *T'oung Pao* XXXIII (1937), pp., 299–300.

"Kuei-ku-tzŭ, the Philosopher of the Ghost Vale," in *China* XII–XIII (1938), pp. 261–272. [Van Gulik's annotated translation of this text was lost during the war; he never returned to it].

"On three antique lutes," in *Transactions of the Asiatic Society of Japan*, 2nd series, vol. XVII (Tokyo; 1938), pp. 155–191; ills.

Critical review of H. Proesent & W. Haenisch, *Bibiographie von Japan*, Bd. V. (Leipzig; 1937), in *Transactions of the Asiatic Society of Japan*, 2nd series, vol. XVII (1938).

"琴銘の研究," in *Sho-en* 書苑 [a Japanese monthly devoted to calligraphy and paleography] pp. 10–16.

"Kakkaron 隔鞾論, a Japanese echo of the opium war," in *Monumenta Serica* IV (1940), pp. 478–545, with 2 plates.

Review of Karl Haushofer, *Geopolitik des Pazifischen Ozeans*, in *Monumenta Serica* V (1940), pp. 485–486.

Review of the Peking edition (1939) of J.O.P. Bland and E. Blackhouse, *China under the Empress Dowager,* in *Monumenta Serica* V (1940), pp. 486–492.

"On the seal representing the god of literature on the title-pages of Chinese and Japanese popular editions," in *Monumenta Nipponica* IV (1941), pp. 33–52.

"Dr. John C. Ferguson's 75th anniversary," in *Monumenta Serica* VI (1941), pp. 340–356, including a bibliography of Ferguson's works.

"The lore of the Chinese lute—addenda and corrigenda," in *Monumenta Nipponica* VII (1951), pp. 300–310, ills.

"Brief note on the *cheng*, the small Chinese cither," in *Tōyō ongaku kenkyū* 東洋音樂研究 9 (1951), pp. 10–25, ills.

"The mango trick in China; an essay on Taoist magic," in *Transactions of the Asiatic Society of Japan* III, 3rd series (1954), pp. 117–175.

"*Yin-ting* 銀釘 and *yin-ting* 銀錠," in *Oriens Extremus* II (1955), pp. 204–205.

"A note on ink cakes," in *Monumenta Nipponica* XI (1955), pp. 84–100.

And there were probably many more. I wouldn't estimate the total number of his titles: dissertations, novels, articles, essays, literary or sinological tidbits, *et. al.* A truly busy man always finds time and van Gulik liked to visit printers, preferably in small shops that would do bookbinding as well, in some backpart of a city he happened to live in or be visiting at the time. As he could always speak the language, no matter where he might find himself, van Gulik habitually succeeded in establishing a mutually beneficial relationship. It also helped that he could print and bind books himself, knew all about typesetting, paper, glue, and what not. By cooperating with these newfound friends a number of small volumes were born, in Beirut, Chungking, The Hague, Tokyo and even Washington. Van Gulik usually happened to have a subject in mind, and could produce a text at a few days' notice, so, if the printer was willing, a limited edition could be set up forthwith. The order had a condition; that the ambassador could help with production, and van Gulik would roll up his sleeves, chew a cigar, tell jokes in Chinese, Arabic, Malay, Japanese, if need be, Dutch, borrow an apron and peruse the available supply of inks. The printers would find that they could learn from their assistant, like the Malaysian man who, up till van Gulik's first visit, had never printed anything but cinema tickets. Most of these books and pamphlets, manufactured in editions of maybe two hundred copies, were lost in due course. Wars raged and revolutions rumbled, van Gulik was transferred or was repatriated. On several occasions he had to leave whatever he owned behind. Twice he lost an entire art collection and his private libraries. When he did have the chance to distribute his production, marketing was not too commercially arranged. He might use his limited stock to serve as useful presents, to friends, relations and colleagues all over the world, and mail them off in time for Christmas and New Year. He also sometimes placed them on consignment with local stores, and even hired soldiers (like during the U.S. occupation of Japan) who might sell them on commission. The business was never profitable in money.

One of these beautifully printed booklets happened to come my way, finding my hand on an Amsterdam street stall. It numbers 32 pages and is called *New Year's Eve in Lan-fang*. Printed in Beirut, on high quality paper, with perfect binding and an elegant lettertype, it may have been created by a monk, moonlighting in the 'Imprimerie catholique.' The illustrations were drawn by van Gulik himself—consisting of two stylized Chinese characters (each in one unbroken line), the one on the left meaning *Fu* (to be happy) and the one on the right saying *Shou* (long life). Together the two symbols from the traditional Chinese wish for a Happy New Year.

What a man, John Blofeld said about van Gulik, and called him a shining example of how not to waste one's timespan here. To be efficiently of use—a tough assignment for most of us, but van Gulik kept passing all his tests *cum laude*. Incense smoulders in front of his portrait.

BIOGRAPHICAL NOTES

1910   9th of August, born in Zutphen, The Netherlands. His father, Willem Jacobus van Gulik, is a physician in the Royal Netherlands East Indies Army.

1915   His first overseas journey, together with his mother and younger sister. WW I is on, but the Netherlands are neutral. The ship sails to Java where he joins his father who traveled ahead for a second tour of service.

1916–1922 Elementary school in Surabaya and Batavia (now Jakarta), Java. He is taught in Dutch but he picks up Malay and Javanese from the servants and in the street. He becomes involved in a lifelong affair with all things Chinese.

1923–1929 Back in The Netherlands (in Nymegen) he studies at a select High School, a 'Gymnasium,' where Latin and Greek are added to a program of modern languages, mathematics and science. His longing for the beautiful island of Java inspires literary work published in *Rostra*, the school's monthly paper. Some of the sketches are in Dutch, some in French. He takes private lessons from a Chinese student in order to perfect his knowledge of written and spoken Cantonese and Mandarin. He meets Professor C.C. Uhlenbeck who teaches him Russian and Sanskrit, and helps his teacher to compile a dictionary of the American Blackfoot Indian language.

In 1928, still as a high school student, he begins to contribute to the scholarly magazine *China*, published by the Dutch Chinese Cultural Association. His well constructed and erudite essays on ancient Chinese poetry are enthusiastically received.

1929–1934 He studies Colonial Oriental law, 'Indology' (a discipline centered on the culture of the then Netherlands Indies), and, of course, Chinese (and Japanese) language and literature, at the famous University of Leyden.

Translates (1932) a play from Sanskrit and manages to have this work published.

Chinese associates give him the name *Gao Lo-pei* (高羅佩) that he will use throughout his further career.

He begins his daily ritual, kept up during the rest of his life, of practising Chinese calligraphy with a brush.

His baccalaureate thesis (1933) appears in English, and is entitled *The Development of the Juridical Position of the Chinese in the Netherlands Indies.*

He transfers to the University of Utrecht to add Tibetan and Sanskrit to his studies and submits his lengthy essay *Mi Fu on inkstones* as his master's thesis.

His Ph.D. (1935) is granted *cum laude* on his dissertation *Hayagriva, mantrayanic aspects of horsecult in China and Japan*, a treatise that deals with esoteric Buddhism.

1935–1942 His first official and diplomatic assignment to the Dutch embassy in Tokyo, Japan. He helps found *Monumenta Nipponica* (1938), at Sophia University, where he will serve as a board member for almost thirty years.

Publishes two studies related to early Chinese ideology concerned with an exotic way of making music. Builds up a library of books and manuscripts on Chinese music, that he loses, together with his first art collection, when WW II breaks out and he is evacuated with Allied diplomatic personnel.

1943   Temporary appointments in East Africa, Egypt and New Delhi, India.

1943–1946 Promoted to First Secretary, at the Dutch Legation, Chungking, the capital of Free China. Plays the Chinese seven stringed lute and makes many high-placed and artistic friends.

Meets and marries Shui Shifang, a graduate of Ch'i-lu University, daughter of an imperial mandarin, and a typist at the Embassy, on December 18, 1943. There are two ceremonies, Protestant and modern Chinese. Willem, the couple's first son, is born the next year. There will be three more children, a daughter and two sons.

Van Gulik becomes interested in book printing and scroll mounting.

1946–1947 Transferred to The Hague, The Netherlands, where he works in the Political Affairs Section of the Ministry of Foreign Affairs. Spends as much time as possible at Leyden University.

He is sent to the U.S. as a counselor at the Dutch Embassy in Washington, D.C. Is appointed as a member of the Far Eastern Commission, advising in matters re the occupation of Japan.

Makes use of U.S. university facilities to further his education in Far Eastern culture.

1948–1951 Is appointed as adviser to the Netherlands Military Mission in Kyoto, Japan. Advises against the Japanese major language reform that will reduce the number of current characters to 1,850 specimens. Nobody listens and he sets out writing the Judge Dee saga. The first book is his translation of an authentic Chinese eighteenth century detective novel, that he has privately printed. The *Dee Goong An, three murder cases solved by Judge Dee*, is a success. Studies Ming style pictorial art in order to be able to illustrate his books authentically himself. In order to satisfy growing demand he writes *The Chinese Bell Murders*, his first original Judge Dee book. The book sells well in English and Dutch, and also in his own Chinese and Japanese versions. Ultimately there will be sixteen books in the series.

As naked women on bookcovers will stimulate sales, his publishers ask for attractive drawings. Van Gulik's search for the genuine Chinese female nude prompts an in-depth investigation that will culminate in the scholarly works *Erotic Coloor Prints of the Ming Period* and *Sexual Life in Ancient China*.

1951–1953 Appointed as counsellor at the Dutch Embassy in New Delhi, India. Continues his studies in Sanskrit and writes his important essay *Siddam*—referring to scholarly work on Sanskrit in Japan and China—that will be published in 1956. The Siddam alphabet of Sanskrit is popular in the type of calligraphy appearing in Japanese esoteric Buddhist art.

1953–1956 Is promoted to director of the Bureau of Middle Eastern and African Affairs in the Ministry of Foreign Affairs. Finds time to study plots for more Judge Dee books. Finds a copy of a thirteenth century handbook for Chinese magistrates, the *Parallel cases under the pear-tree*, that he translates, and has published with his notes and comments.

1956–1959 Promoted to Envoy Extraordinary and Plenipotentiary of The Netherlands to the Middle East, and settles in Beirut, Lebanon. The political situation is most unstable and the assignment therefore dangerous, but van Gulik enjoys his studies in Arabic language and religion at the local university. When his house was bombed, his family evacuated, but van

Gulik continued his work and studies in the basement. He wrote *The Chinese Nail Murders*, vainly in-
tending the book to finish the Judge Dee series. He
also found time to write a monumental work on Chinese art appreciation, *Chinese pictorial art as viewed
by the connoisseur*.

1959–1962 A transfer to Kuala Lumpur, Malaysia, where, at age
forty-nine, he was appointed as Ambassador. He also
became a professor, for he officially lectured at the
University of Malaya. He discovered the agile and
superior gibbons, long-limbed tree apes found in
many parts of the Far East. Several of these graceful
and intelligent beings became his house and garden
pets and he was inspired to collect all available material on this special race of advanced fellow beings.

1963–1964 Another spell in The Hague, The Netherlands, where
he worked as director of the Research and Documen-
tation Bureau of the Ministry of Foreign Affairs.
Writes his only 'Dutch' novel about a lonely man in a
wet raincoat who suffers continuous and painful
defeat, but there's a sur-happy ending when Mr.
Hendriks solves his Zen koan.

1965–1967 Culmination of his diplomatic career with the appointment as Ambassador to Japan and Korea.
Hoping that he would be able to continue his research, he had his complete library shipped to
Tokyo. When his art collection arrived as well, his
official residence was filled to the roof. He still managed to find room for his delicate and friendly gibbons. His treatise *The Gibbon in China* was finished
with some haste as his health degenerated rapidly.
Lung cancer was suspected and confirmed in a The
Hague hospital, where he died, September 24, 1967,
saying to one of his last visitors that he looked forward to whatever was waiting.